# The Tudors

*A Captivating Guide to the History of England from Henry VII to Elizabeth I*

# Free Bonus from Captivating History (Available for a Limited time)

Hi History Lovers!

Now you have a chance to join our exclusive history list so you can get your first history ebook for free as well as discounts and a potential to get more history books for free! Simply visit the link below to join.

Captivatinghistory.com/ebook

Also, make sure to follow us on:

Twitter: @Captivhistory

Facebook: Captivating History:@captivatinghistory

# Contents

# Introduction

Five Tudor monarchs sat on the throne of England and Ireland from 1485 to 1603. The family earned their royal rights through strategic planning and battlefield prowess, and kept them because of intellect, strength and sheer determination. The Tudors, one of England's most powerful and famous royal dynasties, knitted together a fragmented and small island nation that became one of the world's financial, colonial and technological superpowers. There is so much more to the story of these kings and queens than beheadings, political marriages and the reformation of the church – but those events remain some of the family's most enthralling moments.

# Chapter 1 – The Tudors of Wales

The story of the Tudors begins in the late 12th century, when the family was neither powerful nor famous. In fact, the first Tudors were not even English, but Welsh. The Tudor dynasty traces its beginnings to Ednyfed Fychan, who was born sometime in the late 12th century. A servant of the localized North Welsh monarchy, Fychan made himself and his family indispensable to the Princes of the Kingdom of Gwynedd in Medieval Wales. Officially, he was the Court Seneschal: a soldier in charge of feasts, household ceremonies and occasional judgments within the community – essentially, a steward of the great house. Unofficially, he was the kingdom's most trusted diplomat, and ambassador to the English.

Fychan was intensely loyal to the Llywelyn monarchs of Gwynedd in Wales and was recognized as one of the kingdom's most valuable warriors. At a time when Wales and England were completely independent of one another, grievances and spontaneous land grabs were common and Wales in particular needed to be vigilant. When King John of England sent his own soldiers to conquer Welsh Llywelyn lands, Ednyfed successfully defended his country and took the heads of three English lords home to his ruler.

In thanks, Llywelyn had Ednyfed update his family coat of arms to include three helmeted heads. The Prince's loyal servant received lordships over the lands of Brynffanigl and Criccieth, and was also named Chief Justice of the realm. Ednyfed Fychan was a highly-valued man due to his defense of the kingdom and his work within it. In addition to his estates, titles and royal favors, the most telling gift was his status as a tax-free landowner. At a time when Llywelyn was consolidating the Northern Welsh kingdoms and establishing a system of feudalism throughout the land, tax-free status was only granted to royal family members, clergy and born nobility. Fychan's line of descent was granted the same land rights as the most noble courtier; this was his true entrance into the aristocracy.

To further embed himself and his progeny into the political fabric of the region, Ednyfed Fychan married Princess Gwenllian from South Wales. Through the marriage, Ednyfed became cousins with Llywelyn himself – thus beginning the march of his ancient family towards its own throne. Gwenllian gave birth to six sons, all of whom followed in their father's political footsteps by serving the Kingdom of Gwynedd. The Tudurs were largely soldiers and diplomats whose work took them into the English kingdoms of East Anglia and Wessex regularly. The family became very well known in England, enjoying a noble reception at the courts of kings.

Ednyfed's grandson, Tudur Hen, was the first bearer of the famous Welsh name that would eventually be anglicized into "Tudor". Tudur Hen was the Lord of Penmynydd in Anglesey, North Wales. This stronghold was home to several generations of Tudors, including one of particular importance to the royal dynasty: Owain Tudur.

Owain ap Maredud ap Tudur was born between 1390 and 1400. By the 15th century, the Tudur given name had become a formal part of the family's surname, so that when Owain traveled to England he was called Owen Tudor. Owen was a credit to his forebears in every way, except that he used his political drive to the benefit of England instead of his ancestral Wales. Where his father had supported the Welsh revolt against England, Owen Tudor instead sought his fortunes with the powerful oppressor of his homeland.

He ingratiated himself with Henry V, the contemporary English ruler from the house of Lancaster, and became as necessary to the English king as his ancestor had been to the Prince of Gwynedd. Many of the stories of Owen Tudor and King Henry V have fallen into legend, but early biographers claim that the former fought in the king's army and joined the royal retinue at court in 1415 as a royal steward. Tudor is said to have served the king's wife, Queen Catherine of Valois, by bringing her meals and tasting her dishes before she ate. Medieval royalty was always paranoid about being poisoned, so their most-trusted courtiers were required to eat from the royal plates in case the food had been tampered with. Tudor's role as the queen's taster belies his history with – and fierce loyalty for – the king and his family.

When Owen Tudor joined the royal court, Henry V was beginning a massive military campaign against the French. For nearly one hundred years, the House of Plantagenet—of which Henry V was a member—had fought the House of Valois for control of France. In the fall of 1415, Henry V's outnumbered army won a dramatic victory over the French at the Battle of Agincourt. Over the next several years, Henry would go on to conquer Normandy and its capital Rouen, one of the most prosperous cities in Europe. By August of 1419, his army was at the gates of Paris.

The French were in a precarious position. They had suffered significant military defeats, and the kingdom's noble families were preoccupied with intrigue and infighting. The Duke of Burgundy, a member of the Valois family, believed an alliance with the English was in the country's best interested. He persuaded King Charles VI and Queen Isabeau to sign the Treaty of Troyes, which proclaimed Henry V, rather than their own son Charles, and Henry's future sons as the rightful heirs to the French throne. To solidify Henry's claim, he was married to Charles and Isabeau's daughter, Catherine of Valois.

Henry and Catherine's son Henry was born in December 1421, but Henry V's good fortunes were at their end. In August 1422, he died suddenly in France, leaving England with an infant king. Before dying from apparent dysentery, Henry had named his brother, John, English regent until his son was old enough to rule independently. The nine-month-old King of England was also the grandchild and heir to the reigning King Charles VI of France through his mother Catherine of Valois, and through the Treaty of Troyes. With Charles VI's death in October 1422, Henry VI inherited France, as well as England, before his first birthday.

After Henry V's death, Owen Tudor remained in service to Henry VI and his regent. His proximity to the Crown gave him ample opportunity to draw the notice of Queen Catherine, who was nine years his junior. Despite his Welsh royal blood, Tudor was still considered a simple courtier in England. Until 1432, he was not even afforded the "Rights of an Englishman." Nevertheless, Tudor and Catherine became lovers. Whether they married or not is unknown, but they had three sons: Edmund, Jaspar and Edward. There was at least one daughter, Margaret, and perhaps others—few records regarding unmarried women were kept in the fifteenth century.

In mixing his blood with that of the French heiress, Owen Tudor solidified the standing of his children and their descendants as noble and royal. However, a law had been enacted to prevent the dowager queen from remarrying without the consent of the ruling king; Henry VI could not officially consent until he reached the age of sixteen. Therefore, when Catherine died young in 1437, Owen Tudor was arrested and jailed for breaking this law.

Two years later, Owen Tudor received a royal pardon and was given his lands and titles back by King Henry VI, who had reached the age of majority. He also was gifted an annual pension of forty pounds and remained a vital part of the English king's household until 1450. A decade later, he returned to Wales to fight in the Wars of the Roses on the side of the ruling Lancasters. At the Battle of Mortimer's Cross, Tudor was captured and brought before Edward of York. Expecting merely to be taken hostage, Tudor realized moments before his beheading that he was going to die. His last words were rather romantic:

*"That hede shalle ly on the stocke that wass wonte to ly on Quene Katheryns lappe. [sic]"*

# Chapter 2 – The Wars of the Roses

Owen Tudor could not have predicted that the war which took his life would, one day, make kings of his descendants. His two sons who lived to adulthood, Edmund and Jasper, were treated well by King Henry VI, their half-brother. Edmund, the elder brother, was made the first Earl of Richmond in 1452. But it was Edmund's marriage to twelve-year-old Margaret Beaufort in 1455 that would set the Tudors on the path to the crown.

In 1437, Henry VI reached age sixteen and assumed responsibility for England. He displayed a true desire for his role as monarch; however, his character and beliefs about the kingdom differed from his father's. Henry, like many kings before him, was burdened by the Hundred Years' War between England and France. During Henry VI's regency period, the English had lost traction in France. Instead of ramping up military efforts as was the advice of his council, the king wanted to foster a new era of peace between the nations.

The king was convinced that, in order to begin a time of peace with France, he should marry the niece of French King Charles VII, Margaret of Anjou. The bride was fifteen years old when she married the thirty-four-year-old King of England in 1445. Though young, Margaret was focused and political. She made sure that her new husband followed through on his promise to transfer the French province of Maine back to the French crown.

The land transfer was a divisive issue among the English nobility, which had already grown fragmented during the childhood of their boy-king. But by 1450, a far more pressing issue had emerged: after five years of marriage, Henry VI still had no heir. To make matters worse, the king struggled with bouts of insanity. With a weak king and no obvious heir, several candidates for the throne began jockeying for power.

Two families—the Beauforts and the Yorks—could both trace their ancestry to Edward III, who had ruled England from 1327 to 1377. As members of the House of Plantagenet, both families held claim to the throne. Like Henry VI, the Beauforts belonged to the Lancastrian line, and aligned themselves with the king. Richard of York, however, saw in the king's illness an opportunity to expand his own power. In 1453, Margaret was finally pregnant, but Henry's instability prevented him from governing. Richard successfully maneuvered to make himself Lord Protector—essentially, the regent of England during Henry's incapacity.

Henry had sufficiently improved by 1455 to arrange a promising marriage for Edmund Tudor. Margaret Beaufort had previously been married at the age of 9 to John de la Pole, but this political pairing was annulled to allow for the match between Henry's Tudor half-brother and the daughter of his cousin and prominent ally: John Beaufort, 1st Duke of Somerset. Almost immediately after the marriage, Edmund Tudor departed for a diplomatic mission to Wales. The visit was successful until, back in England, the political strife between the Lancasters and the Yorks erupted into military conflict at the Battle of St. Albans. Richard of York claimed victory over the royal army, led by Margaret Beaufort's uncle Edward. King Henry was captured, and Richard cemented his power as Lord Protector.

The War of the Roses had begun. For over thirty years, the Lancaster and York families battled each other for the throne of England. The name of the war is a poetic reference to the emblems of both parties: the red rose of the Lancasters and the white rose of the Yorks.

Edmund Tudor was an early casualty of the war. Soon after the Battle of St. Albans, Richard's son Edward York sent thousands of troops into Wales to assert his authority. Edmund was captured and imprisoned and died shortly thereafter of the bubonic plague. The same Edward of York would order Owen Tudor's beheading in 1460.

Upon Edmund's death, young Margaret Beaufort, Countess of Richmond and Derby, became a thirteen-year-old widow. Two months later, on January 28, 1457, she became the mother of the future Tudor king. The infant Henry was directly related to the Welsh royal houses through his paternal grandfather Owen Tudor, the French House of Valois through his paternal grandmother Catherine of Valois, and the English ruling Lancasters of the House of Plantagenet through his mother; in terms of bloodlines, Henry Tudor was a genuine candidate for the English throne.

Unlike his half-uncle Henry VI, Henry Tudor would be no boy-king. In the first three decades of his life, four other men claimed the throne. After a second battle at St. Albans—in which Edward of York, like his father before him, claimed victory—Henry VI fled to Scotland with Margaret, and Edward assumed the throne as Edward IV. In 1470, Margaret forged a secret alliance with two of Edward IV's main supporters, allowing her husband to regain his throne. But Henry's victory was short-lived; the following year, the king was captured by Yorkist soldiers and imprisoned in the Tower of London. He died there one month later, presumably murdered on the order of Edward IV, who had regained power.

Edward retained the throne until his death in 1483, when his son, Edward V, replaced him. The younger Edward was captured by the followers of Richard III, Edward IV's brother, and disappeared at the age of twelve. Despite the fact that both Edward and Richard were of the House of York, the latter decided to seize the throne for his own purposes, not that of the York cause.

Richard III installed himself as the King of England in 1483, but his grasp on the throne was uneasy. Henry Tudor, among thousands of others, had mourned not only the loss of his friend, Henry VI, but the loss of the Lancastrian line. After the death of Henry's son Edward of Westminster in 1471, the Lancaster family was without heirs, making a Yorkish king the only sensible option for England.

Unless, of course, there were one more option that had heretofore been overlooked: the legitimate claim of Henry Tudor. With no Lancaster to fight for, Henry let the idea of kingship ruminate in his brain for fourteen years, which he spent in the relative safety of Brittany. After the death of twelve-year-old Edward V, Tudor decided it was time to heed his mother's advice and pursue the throne for himself.

Tudor traveled westward, gathering an army as he did so. In his birth country, Tudor found immense support for his bid to the throne. Henry already possessed the Lancastrian bloodline necessary to challenge Richard of York, but he made his potential kingship even more enticing for the English when he promised to make a York woman his queen. When he met Richard III and the York soldiers on the battlefield at Bosworth Field, Henry had amassed 5,000 soldiers for his cause. In addition, his army was supplied by Brittany and France.

On the 22nd of August, 1485, the Tudor and York armies met between Leicester and Market Bosworth in England. The royal army outnumbered Tudor's by an estimated 3,000 soldiers, but Richard didn't count on the treason of two of his trusted men: Lord Stanley and his brother, Sir William Stanley. Perhaps he should have, since the former was married to none other than Margaret Beaufort, Henry Tudor's own mother. When the battle began, Lord Stanley remained inactive, while his brother joined directly with the opposing Tudor ranks.

Even so outnumbered, the Tudor army managed to out-maneuver their opposition. Richard fought fiercely, gunning for his primary foe straight from the beginning of the battle. Before he could engage Henry with his sword, however, the Tudor army surrounded and killed the king.

With Richard dead, Henry Tudor proudly pronounced himself the King of England. True to his word, he married Elizabeth of York, thus joining the warring families of York and Lancaster together on the throne. The Battle of Bosworth Field was the final major battle of the Wars of the Roses. The triumph inspired a lengthy poem in praise of King Henry VII and those who helped his cause:

*"Sir Perciuall Thriball, the other hight,*
*& noble Knight, & in his hart was true;*
*King Richards standard hee kept vpright*
*vntill both his leggs were hewen him froe;*

*the ground he wold neuer lett itt goe,*
*whilest the breath his brest ws within;*
*yett men pray ffor the Knights 2*
*that euer was soe true to their King.*

*then they moued to a mountaine on height,*
*with a lowde voice they cryed king HENERY,*
*the crowne of gold that was bright,*
*to the Lord stanley deliuered itt bee. [sic]"*

To commemorate the end of three decades of civil war, King Henry VII created his new emblem: the Tudor rose, with red and white petals. It was the beginning of the infamous Tudor dynasty that would see England into the modern age.

# Chapter 3 – Catherine of Valois, Mother of the Tudor Dynasty

Catherine of Valois was born to Charles VI, King of France, and Isabella of Bavaria in 1401 in Paris. She was educated at a convent outside of the capital city and provided with religious texts throughout her childhood. Daughter of a great monarchy, she was considered an important bargaining chip in European politics – particularly with regard to England.

While Catherine was still a child, her parents seriously considered betrothing her to the English Prince of Wales, Henry Plantagenet (Lancaster), but the English king died in 1413, before negotiations could be settled. Of his own volition, young Henry decided to pursue the marriage once more after he ascended the throne. Having never met Catherine, his interest in her was purely political and aimed at consolidating England with several English-occupied regions of France.

As the marriage talks continued, so too did Henry V's military campaigns in France. The English king recaptured Agincourt, a much-contested piece of land in the north-eastern part of modern France. Much was made of Henry's accomplishments abroad and all his successors would try to find similar glory for themselves, only to be disappointed. Once he had captured the region in the name of England in October of 1415, King Henry V put his energy into reaching a peaceful agreement with France that would be to his own benefit.

Charles VI of France eventually agreed to Henry's terms of peace, including that the English king would be named heir to the throne of France. In order for this incredible stipulation to make sense for the Valois family, Charles arranged for his daughter to marry Henry V and become the Queen of England. She did so in France on June 2, 1420, at the age of nineteen. Once the newlyweds arrived in England, King Henry started planning a lavish coronation ceremony for Catherine that took place in February of the next year.

Despite having achieved so much with France, Henry V went back to the mainland to push for even more land. He died from illness while abroad, leaving the English throne to his infant son who was less than a year old. Catherine of Valois was widowed at the age of 21 and given the relationship between herself, France and England; she probably expected to rule England as regent for her tiny son Henry VI. Such an arrangement would have made a lot of sense; Catherine was the boy's only remaining parent and she strengthened the ties between her son and the French throne. However, Henry V, after becoming very ill, had designated his brother, Humphrey of Lancaster, as Lord Protector over the child king. Henry V's other brother, John of Lancaster, was appointed Regent of France.

There are two possibilities when it comes to explaining why Henry VI's mother was overlooked as regent. The first is that Catherine was simply too French to be considered an appropriate regent over England. Though the two countries had reached an important agreement at that point, it was still possible that Catherine and her father, King Charles VI, might overturn the original treaty and make England a political annex of France.

The second reason is that Catherine's father was a known sufferer of mental illness. He displayed a number of symptoms of delusion, including the tendency to race from room to room insisting that enemies were pursuing him. He also forgot about the existence of his wife and children from time to time and believed that he was made of glass. This sickness ran in his family and would affect Henry VI, Catherine's own son. Perhaps, to Henry V, it was unwise to leave the two kingdoms in the hands of a family whose most remarkable virtue was that of madness. Catherine of Valois did not have any sort of mental illness herself, but it would have been an easy issue to bring up if she were given any sort of real power over King Henry VI.

So, upon the death of her husband the king, Catherine became the Dowager Queen of England. In title she was the most noble mother of the king but, in reality, Catherine struggled to find firm footing in a country that was not her own. She was still young, attractive, and of royal blood, so suitors were not in short supply. The man she chose, however, was something of a surprise. Catherine chose to marry the man who'd been one of her closest servants: Owen Tudor.

The two became grandparents to Henry Tudor, the man who would fight King Richard III for the crown of England and end the Wars of the Roses. Perhaps unknowingly, Catherine of Valois had become part of the family who would rule England for three centuries. Her Tudor husband and children went on to defend the crown on behalf of her first son, King Henry VI, and when Henry was murdered in the Tower of London, they took control for themselves.

For Catherine, her ultimate loyalty was for her children, both Henry VI and her Tudor sons, Edmund and Jasper. Though Henry VI was weak, mentally ill, and not suited for the kingship he inherited from his royal father and grandfather, Catherine worked hard to create a strong family unit around the young king and herself. Owen and the Tudor children rallied around their mother, their father, and the Lancaster king, who offered them favors and beneficial marriages when he was able.

It was because of this secondary family unit, centered around Catherine of Valois, that the Tudor dynasty had the bloodlines and the familial strength to take over from the Plantagenet line of kings.

Due to the need of the displaced French princess to forge her way ahead and make a stable life for herself, Queen Catherine was a formidable Tudor woman without whom the bulk of English history would be very different. If not for the character, hard work, and motherly support of Catherine of Valois, the Tudor men would not have possessed the ability to accomplish what they did.

# Chapter 4 – Margaret Beaufort, Second Tudor Matriarch

The men who established the post-Plantagenet line of English kings would have done very little had it not been for the powerful, motivated women behind the scenes. Margaret Beaufort was one of the primary forces behind the formation of the powerful Tudor family within England, and the first female member of the Tudors whose ambition was channeled into their eventual rise to power.

Born around the year 1443 in Bletsoe Castle, Margaret was descended from John of Gaunt through her father, who was Gaunt's illegitimate grandson. The connection was too tenuous for Margaret or her father to claim the throne, but it was remembered nonetheless and the family was very close to King Henry VI. Margaret was the only surviving child of her father, John Beaufort, and her mother, Margaret Beauchamp, which meant that she inherited a great deal of money and land when John died. Unfortunately, since Margaret was only a baby at the time of her inheritance, her property and fortune was placed in the wardship of William de la Pole, the first Duke of Suffolk.

Margaret was used as a pawn in two marriage plots to get control of her lands and money, both of which occurred during her early childhood. To keep Beaufort's wealth in his control, William de la Pole had his son John marry Margaret sometime between the years 1444 and 1450. She was no more than three years old at the time of the wedding, but John de la Pole was probably only one year old himself. The marriage was annulled three years later when William de la Pole was killed, and King Henry VI transferred the wardship of Margaret's property to his half-brothers, Jasper and Edmund Tudor. Once more, the girl was married off to one of her patrons: Edmund Tudor. She was 12 and he was 24, and the country had just been thrown into the chaos of the civil war. Edmund fought for his half-brother's Lancastrian forces during the war, and soon after his marriage he was taken prisoner by the Yorkist army. There, he contracted the plague and died.

Margaret was a 13-year-old widow with a newborn son, the first Henry Tudor. She gave birth at her brother-in-law Jasper's residence at Pembroke, Wales, and very nearly lost her own life, as well as that of her baby. Perhaps because she was such a very young mother, and Henry an only child in his mother's care, the two were very loyal and attached to one another. Theirs was a lifelong bond which motivated Margaret to do everything in her power to ensure the best future for her son. She recognized the fact that Henry's safety lay in the hands of his Tudor family, who were so close to the Lancastrian king, and she forever sang the praises of her lost husband, Edmund.

Due to her trust in the Tudor's best intentions for their young relation, Margaret peacefully allowed her young son to remain with family in Wales. There, he was among his ancestral countrymen and far away from the violence and uncertainty of the ongoing Wars of the Roses.

Despite her foresworn loyalty to Edmund and his relations, Margaret married a third time, one year after the birth of Henry. This time, her husband was Henry Stafford, a member of the nobility some 20 years Margaret's senior. She was still a teenager at the time of her third wedding. Possibly due to the difficult labor she'd experienced with Henry, Margaret had no children with Henry Stafford. She did, however, enjoy a reasonably stable marriage to her third husband. She took over the administration of her inherited lands and received Woking Palace from King Henry VI.

Pragmatism alone was an excellent reason to keep young Henry Tudor in Wales, but there was another motive behind the decision. Stafford, oddly, did not support the Lancastrian cause and instead fought for the Yorkists. Margaret perhaps played the role of dutiful Yorkist wife in an effort to keep her enemies – and the enemies of her son – close. When Stafford died fighting for Edward York at the Battle of Barnet, Margaret quickly married for a fourth time to Thomas Stanley. In marrying another York favorite, the Tudor mother gained the ability to serve at the court of England's first York king, Edward IV, and after his death, the court of Richard III.

At court, Margaret kept her eyes and ears open. She was taking care of Henry from afar by staying abreast of the gossip and news from the changing English royals. She found the co-conspirator she needed in Elizabeth Woodville, the widow of Edward IV and mother of the princes presumed murdered by usurper Richard III. The two women both had significant reasons to desire the overthrow of the new king and soon became embroiled in an elaborate and dynamic plot.

The two women are historically implicated in Buckingham's Rebellion of October 1483, as well as the idea to marry Henry Tudor to a York princess. The rebellions were unsuccessful but the marriage plan was not. Margaret and Elizabeth both wanted to play up Henry Tudor's Lancastrian bloodline to boost him to the throne, but they were smart enough to realize one bloodline alone wouldn't be enough to put an end to the constant succession of kings or rebellions. Henry needed to marry into the York family to create the perfect mixture of Lancaster and York.

Margaret Beaufort was not the only one who believed in such a plan. In fact, Richard III was rumored to have seriously considered marrying Elizabeth of York after the death of his wife Anne. It would have served him well in terms of consolidating his power with that of his dead brother, but his plan lacked the vital element that Margaret, Elizabeth Woodville, and the Tudor family's featured: the connection of the two Plantagenet bloodlines. Furthermore,

Elizabeth and her daughter would have been disgusted at the idea of marriage to Richard III – he was the younger Elizabeth's uncle, and believed to be the murderer of her young brothers.

The Tudors and the widowed Queen Elizabeth Woodville, with full support of Margaret despite her marriage to a Yorkist, put together fresh armies prior to the Battle of Bosworth. Jasper and Henry Tudor had significant support from France and Wales that bolstered their numbers, and Margaret's husband failed to declare loyalty to either side. Since he was traditionally a York supporter, this was a great success for Margaret and Henry's coup. The plan succeeded, and it was Margaret Beaufort's husband, Lord Stanley, who placed Richard III's lost crown upon the head of his stepson. Both Margaret and Elizabeth had succeeded in placing their children on the throne of England.

With Henry Tudor proclaimed King of England, Margaret's life improved greatly. She was granted titles and authority by her son and called "My Lady the King's Mother" at court. Henry's Parliament allowed her to own lands in her own right, separate from her husband, and even act as a judge in the northern part of the realm. She enjoyed every freedom and luxury during the latter half of her life and remained exceptionally close to the son she'd helped to achieve such greatness. As an older woman, Margaret tired of married life and took a vow of chastity with the Catholic Church. Her husband, Lord Stanley, was peaceful concerning the decision, and often visited his wife though she lived apart from him.

At the end of Margaret Beaufort's life, she was the most powerful woman in England. Her body was interred next to that of Edmund Tudor, the father King Henry VII never knew.

# Chapter 5 – King Henry VII

Henry Tudor was born, like his ancestors, in Wales. His claim to the English throne was legitimate but tenuous: His royal English bloodline came from his mother instead of his father, and he was possibly illegitimate. Nevertheless, the descendant of Ednyfed Fychan of Gwynedd became King Henry VII of England and France and Lord of Ireland on the 22nd of August, 1485.

To prevent uprisings by the vanquished Yorks, the new king was fair with the remaining members of the family and their supporters. Henry spared both the life and the lands of Richard III's heir, the Earl of Lincoln. Furthermore, the king made it clear that any man who had fought alongside the Yorks would be pardoned so long as he swore an oath of loyalty.

The self-proclaimed king also recognized the wisdom of forestalling a meeting with the English parliament until he had strengthened his claim to the throne. In October of 1485, Henry celebrated his kingship with a coronation ceremony at Westminster Abby. The following January, he was married to Elizabeth of York in the same venue. These important royal tasks accomplished, King Henry VII met with his parliament and began the daily work of running the Kingdom of England and Ireland, as well as England's lands in France.

Henry immediately began to implement changes that would discourage any continuation of the Wars of the Roses. One of the first practices he outlawed was the nobility's keeping of immense livery and maintenance staff. Such staff were required to wear the emblem of their noble employer and often displayed fierce loyalty to their lord's house. Henry had witnessed many uprisings over the previous thirty years, many due to the fact that a potential candidate for the throne could quickly gather an army of his friend's staff. His claim to the throne insecure, Henry cut off these potential armies at their source.

In addition to stripping the aristocracy of their excessive staff, Henry VII brought in much stricter taxation laws and means of collection. There was very little the nobility could do to avoid this increased taxation: Henry's laws stated that if a noble house spent excessively, it must be able to afford higher taxes. On the other hand, law also stated that if a noble house spent little, it could also afford higher taxes because its income must be saved. In this way, Henry VII refilled the royal coffers and eventually calmed the incessant rebellions of nobles who believed they had a legitimate claim to the throne.

This restriction of the nobility was one of the most important strategies the king employed during his reign. There were, nevertheless, continued uprisings in the first years of Henry's reign. Various claimants to the English and Irish thrones gathered supporters and attacked Henry's armies over the course of the next decade. In 1486, 1487, 1491, 1495 and 1497 the king was forced to protect himself from would-be usurpers, many of whom had blood ties to previous kings just as he did. Henry VII crushed every attempt to steal his throne and continually passed legislation that made it more difficult for any faction of the nobility to hold enough power and staff to challenge him. To further stabilize the kingdom and his position, Henry created the King's Council. These council members were all appointed by the king himself, and therefore a separate entity than the existing English Parliament. Though Henry realized the necessity of meeting with the Parliament, which was essentially a gathering of noble heads of household, he did so as infrequently as possible. Unlike today, the monarchs of the 15<sup>th</sup> and 16<sup>th</sup> centuries could wait years before summoning a Parliamentary meeting. Henry VII preferred to confer with his own council, half clergy and half nobility, while making decisions. The Parliament was generally only necessary when the king wanted to change taxation laws.

Henry's council, unlike Parliament, met frequently. There were as many as 150 councilors at any given time, though slow transportation typically restricted meeting size to about 40 members. As Henry's reign progressed, he sought out the most educated and knowledgeable of his kingdom to join the council. The king required the best minds to assist him with questions of law, feudal land disputes, taxation, finance and myriad other categories of monarchal administration. The nobility was understandably disgruntled by the shifting balance of power in the kingdom, but it was the King's Council that kept Henry better-informed than any recent king.

To maintain his authority outside of London and major cities, Henry appointed a Justice of the Peace in each county to act as local law enforcement. The job was unpaid, but the stature and power involved appealed to members of the nobility. This kingdom-wide network of law and order was unprecedented.

As Henry brought the most serious in-fighting amongst English nobility to an end, he began to turn his attention to important matters beyond England's shores. Like his predecessor, Henry VI, Henry Tudor wanted peace and prosperity for his kingdom. In the late 15<sup>th</sup> century, this meant directing his foreign policy towards Spain and France.

The latter half of the 15<sup>th</sup> century was a tumultuous period on the Iberian peninsula. The marriage of Isabella I of Castille and Ferdinand II of Aragon in 1469 united Iberia's two most powerful Christian kingdoms and provided the framework for expansion. Isabella and Ferdinand were a power couple. In 1478, they conquered the Canary Islands. In January 1492 they oversaw the conclusion of the Reconquista with the victory over the Emirate of Granada, the last Muslim kingdom in Iberia. Later that month, they funded Christopher Columbus' voyages to the west, the first steps towards the creation of a massive Spanish empire in the Americas.

Henry VII wanted to cement a positive relationship with the new Kingdom of Spain as soon as possible. In 1489, he entered into an agreement with Isabella and Ferdinand that saw his eldest son, Arthur, married to their eldest daughter, Catherine. In addition, the Treaty of Medina del Campo promised that England would come to Spain's aid against France, if ever the need arose.

Henry's dealings with France, just three years later, were somewhat problematic given his prior agreements with Spain. Though the ruler of England believed himself to inherit the French throne, most England's holdings in France had been lost by the time Henry VII became king. Since England and Ireland were struggling financially, the king proposed a solution to the problems of war and money with one document: The Peace of Etaples. The treaty was signed by Henry Tudor and French King Charles VIII on November 3, 1492. The Peace of Etaples signified the end of England's invasions of French lands. The English conceded French ownership of Brittany and, in exchange, France agreed to pay Henry 742,000 crowns at the rate of 50,000 crowns per year. It was a huge financial win for Henry, who in signing the document increased the annual income of the crown by 50 percent. Henry's diplomatic skill led to a comfortable co-existence with France for the remainder of his reign.

The last decade of Henry VII's life and rule were the most emotionally difficult. His eldest son and heir to the throne, Arthur, had married Catherine of Aragon, but died mere months after the wedding took place. Distraught, the usually placid King Henry VII wept over his son's death. One year later, the death of his wife Elizabeth led him to shut himself in his rooms for days without speaking to anyone.

Following the death of his eldest son and wife, Henry Tudor decided to leave the Tower of London, which had been their family home. His son Henry lived sporadically in the Tower, but it had generally fallen out of favor and was eventually used for everything but long-term housing for kings and queens. After Henry VII's son moved on, the Tower was used as a military base, storage center, armory, prison and tourist attraction, but never again as the home of an English monarch.

Henry remained close to his young mother for his entire life, allowing her a gentle hand at court and in royal proceedings. Addressed as My Lady the King's Mother, Margaret remarried several times after the death of Edmund Tudor, but her will declared her desire to be buried alongside her second husband.

The king died of tuberculosis on April 21, 1509, having remained unmarried after the death of Elizabeth. His mother, the young widow of Edmund Tudor who bore her son at the tender age of thirteen, died two months later. Her death came one day after the eighteenth birthday of her only living grandson, heir to the English throne: Henry VIII.

# Chapter 6 – Arthur Tudor

Henry VII was a clever man who was very aware of the role symbolism played in the hearts of the English people. He was, after all, the king who created the melded Tudor rose to unite the Houses of York and Lancaster, and who married a York to compliment his Lancastrian bloodline. He wanted to create a powerful, almost mythical story around his family and his reign so that he would be respected, feared, and beloved in equal measure. With the birth of his son, Henry continued to weave together his tale, pulling a name from one of the most treasured stories in English history: King Arthur and the Knights of the Round Table.

Though Henry VIII would ultimately inherit the throne from his namesake, the eldest boy born to King Henry VII and Elizabeth of York was actually Arthur Tudor. Born in September 1486, Arthur was the first child born of the union between the York and Lancastrian lines. He enjoyed all the best that his kingly father could give him and was the first in a long succession of Tudor princes and princesses who were provided for lavishly during their childhoods.

Arthur's entire childhood was focused on two things: His education and the future marital alliance of England and Spain. The boy received the best tutors and probably the most comprehensive education any royal child had ever had in England. John Reed, Thomas Linacre, and Bernard Andre were responsible for most of the prince's studies. These and other teachers taught him Greek, Latin, writing and reading, ethics, rhetoric, and history, as well as the sports and military knowledge that were becoming of an heir to the throne of one of Europe's great monarchies. He was also very well-versed in the laws and philosophies of Roman Catholicism. Arthur was a good student whose particular aptitudes lay in Greek philosophy, dancing, and archery.

King Henry VII and his queen put a great deal of thought into the future of their eldest son, especially in terms of who might become his wife – and they did so from the moment of his birth. Catherine of Aragon was ultimately chosen as the best mate for Arthur as early as 1488 when the king signed the Treaty of Medina del Campo with Spain. The two countries agreed that Catherine of Aragon would travel to England in 1500 to marry Prince Arthur.

From the time of the betrothal until Catherine embarked upon her long trip to England, both Arthur and his future bride exchanged letters. As the boy aged, he wrote letters to his Spanish fiancée in Latin, a language that both could understand. Catherine wrote back, and at first these letters were stilted and childish. As both the future bride and groom got older, however, the letters became sweet and endearing, with both professing great love for one another. By the time the two were nearing the age of majority, they felt they knew each other quite well despite never having even set eyes upon one another.

Unlike his younger brother Henry, Arthur was a tall and lean boy with a gentle nature. He was not as athletically-inclined as Henry but was still considered fit and handsome by his contemporaries. He had reddish hair like his brother, a trait that is still considered a common family attribute within the English royal family. A contemporary portrait painted when Arthur was probably a teenager shows him with shoulder-length reddish-brown hair, pale skin and brown or hazel eyes.

Prince Arthur was not only a potential political tool in terms of marriage, but in terms of the variety of royal titles and duties he could hold within his own kingdom. His foremost role was as the

Prince of Wales. King Henry VII and his family had their roots in Wales, which made him want to cement his ties there first and foremost. The Tudor Royal Coat of Arms was designed with a red dragon on the left side of the field of Tudor roses, a clear nod to Henry's proud Welsh lineage since that part of the realm had used a dragon as its emblem since at least the 9th century. Henry VII made Arthur the Prince of Wales so that his Welsh neighbors felt connected and respected by their former countryman. As a child, the title pinned to Arthur Tudor was mostly for show, but after he became married his father planned for him to occupy Wales personally. Jasper Tudor, Arthur's uncle, oversaw the administration of the cooperative realms of Wales until that time. It was an important and strategic move on the part of Henry VII. During his reign, entire ancient kingdoms within Wales kneeled to the authority of England.

Prince Arthur had a vast household of servants from all parts of the realm, Wales and Ireland included. Sons of the nobility were sent to his palace to serve their prince in a great variety of ways, including dressing and undressing him, serving his meals, keeping the fires of the palace lit, and keeping inventory of his jewelry. Many of these roles had not existed prior to the rule of Henry VII, who continually developed the proprietary rules of the king's privy chamber throughout his reign.

At one point, Arthur was served by the former Lord Deputy of Ireland following that man's treasonous promotion of Lambert Simnel, pretender to the throne. Simnel had gained a following in Ireland in the latter part of the 1480s for allegedly being the lost Prince Edward Plantagenet, son of King Edward IV. The ruse was enough to incite an uprising led by John de la Pole, Earl of Lincoln, but once Henry's forces overpowered the rebels, the boy was put to work in the kitchens of King Henry VII's castle. Similarly, the false heir's main surviving supporter in Ireland was sent to serve Arthur.

Arthur finally met his bride-to-be in 1501 at the age of 15. The couple was married at St. Paul's Cathedral in London and immediately sent to Ludlow Castle to begin their administration of Wales from the Welsh Marches. Both the young prince and his wife contracted an unidentified illness in March 1502. Catherine of Aragon survived, but in April of 1502, Arthur passed away. His father and mother were heartbroken, both breaking down in tears at the news. They gave their eldest son a magnificent funeral and had his body embalmed and entombed at Worcester Castle in England.

# Chapter 7 – King Henry VIII

Henry VII's son received what may be considered the first example of a classic royal education. He learned from many top-rate tutors and could speak French, Latin and some Italian. He received many royal appointments from his father, who wanted to keep the majority of leadership roles in the family. Though young Henry wanted for nothing and enjoyed an easy childhood in comparison to his older brother Arthur, all responsibility for the future of the family and country fell to him when Arthur died unexpectedly.

When the elder Tudor son died of what was then called "sweating sickness," his marriage to Catherine of Aragon was only a few months old. Still insistent on forging a marital bond between the English and Spanish thrones, Henry VII arranged for Arthur's wedding to be annulled and for Catherine to be newly married to his son Henry. Several complications put off the marriage, but soon after his eighteenth birthday, the new King Henry VIII announced he would go ahead with the wedding.

Henry and Catherine married in June of 1509 at a small ceremony in Greenwich. Two weeks later, the couple celebrated their coronation at Westminster Abby.

Henry VIII was not cautious about beginning his rule. He was clearly of age, married and ready to fill his many palaces with a large collection of royal heirs and spares. Almost immediately after his coronation, Henry set his sights on two of his father's advisors: Richard Empson and Edmund Dudley.

Empson and Dudley had been two of the most prominent members of Henry VII's King's Council. Prominence, however, was not the same as popularity. The public despised Empson and Dudley, as they represented the high tax laws of the former King's Council. The nobility in particular blamed the men for Henry VII's tax increases. The two were charged with treason, found guilty and executed by beheading on Tower Hill.

It was exactly how Henry VIII wanted to introduce his reign. Henry believed in swift, decisive action. He wanted it made clear that he was prepared to have even those closest to him killed if necessary. Not only did the deaths of Empson and Dudley overjoy the masses, they revealed the kind of king that Henry VIII intended to be: a strong, single-minded and ruthless one.

No amount of determination could accomplish for Henry VIII one of his dearest goals: the birth of a son. Queen Catherine became pregnant almost immediately after her marriage to Henry. Sadly, their first child was a stillborn daughter. Only four months after the stillbirth, the queen was pregnant again, and this time she gave birth to a boy. In obvious Tudor fashion, he was called Henry. The much-celebrated royal child, however, only lived for a few weeks. Years passed, and Henry and Catherine experienced two more stillbirths before Princess Mary was born in 1516. She was healthy, vivacious and devoted to her parents.

King Henry had grown up with parents who loved and respected one another, and though Henry VII and Elizabeth of York experienced their share of infant loss, they produced four healthy children. Most importantly, given how lines of succession operated in the late medieval period, they produced two boys. The new King Henry had likely expected to find himself in the same situation as had his parents, but after seven years of marriage he only had one daughter. Furthermore, Queen Catherine was six years older than the king, making her 31 years old after the birth of Mary. Given the environment and time frame in which she lived, Catherine was not expected to remain fertile for much longer, and this worried the king.

With domestic issues weighing on his mind, Henry VIII tried to focus on the administration of the country's foreign affairs. His first problem was with France. Though Henry wanted peaceful relations with his neighbors, as his father had, he was also consumed with the desire to regain all of England's lost lands in France. By the time Henry VIII ascended to the throne, only Calais remained in English hands.

In the early years of Henry's reign, France was allied with the Holy Roman Empire, and therefore much too powerful to even consider provoking. Instead of making demands, Henry met with King Louis XII of France on friendly terms. Immediately afterward, he met with King Ferdinand II to establish himself as an ally of Spain. It was the same political move his father had made, except that Henry VIII intended only to bide his time, keeping peace until it better served his wishes not to do so.

Pope Julius II, meanwhile, had no such concerns about keeping the peace. He drew monarchs across Europe into his wars against his neighbors: first Venice, the once-prosperous but declining republic to the northeast of the Papal States, and later the French, who were encroaching on Lombardy to the north. As the pope's wars drew on, the European monarchs grew weary of the conflict, and anxious to regain lands they had lost along the way. A series of treaty discussions began, into which Henry VIII threw himself wholeheartedly. If European borders were to be redrawn, he wanted some of France for himself – particularly Aquitaine, which had been in English hands for three centuries until it was lost by Henry VI.

To facilitate sympathy for his cause, King Henry pledged military aid to the Pope and his allies in the event of a French attack. True to his word, he sent English troops into Italy when the French launched their counterattacks in 1513. Henry's army was strong, capturing first Therouanne, then Tournai from the French. The king was fiercely dedicated to his task, having been promised the title of "Most Christian King" by the pope himself. Henry's ultimate dream was to be crowned by the pope, in Paris, as king of France.

Meanwhile, at home, Scotland took full advantage of the fact that England's king was overseas. James IV was on the Scottish throne, with Henry's sister Margaret by his side as queen. According to the Auld Alliance of 1295, Scotland and France were pledged in friendship and service to one another. While the English king fought the French directly on the continent, James IV upheld his ancestor's part of the agreement by attacking his southern neighbor.

England was not without a leader, however, nor was she without an army. Henry had left his wife in charge during his absence, and Queen Catherine proved a very capable commander. The Scottish army was ultimately defeated and the king killed in combat before Henry VIII even returned to England.

# Chapter 8 – Margaret Tudor, Sister of Henry VIII

Margaret Tudor, eldest sister of Henry VIII, was the second of Henry VII's children to be strategically matched with a foreign power. She was born in October of 1489, three years after her brother Arthur and two years before Henry. By the time she was 13 years old, Margaret was promised in marriage to King James IV of Scotland. It was an earnest attempt on the part of the English king to join England and Scotland in a peaceful union.

The girl accepted her duty as a princess of the realm and probably quite enjoyed the festivities put on by her father at the time of the proxy wedding in January of 1502. There was feasting, jousting, games, and many gifts to the young queen. She received a brand-new trousseau and Italian bed curtains to bring with her to Edinburgh in summer of 1503 for the official journey. Her friend and Maid of Honor, Lady Catherine Gordon, was also bestowed with fine new clothes befitting her station. Gordon was something of a ward of the English crown at that point, as she'd come from Scotland as the wife of pretender to the throne, Perkin Warbeck. She was one of the only servants to stay with Margaret Tudor after the long journey to Scotland, as was tradition.

Margaret's travel plans were put off until both her father and James IV had exchanged several properties named in the marriage agreement. When the time finally came to leave England, the princess' mother, Elizabeth of York, and her brother Arthur had died. The Tudor household was morose and forlorn, with King Henry struggling to pull himself out of his grief. There was precious little left of the family Margaret had grown up with and loved, a fact that must have made the northward journey particularly bittersweet. She reached the border on August 1 and traveled onward to Dalkeith Castle to rest and prepare for her formal meeting with King James IV the next day.

James, 16 years his bride's senior, was too impatient to wait to meet Margaret now that she was within riding distance. Without bothering to change into formal attire, the king set off for Dalkeith and surprised the young bride in her appointed rooms within the castle. She was dressed for the occasion in a golden dress, though James appeared to have just been hunting. They had an amicable meeting followed by supper and dancing. That night, two of Margaret's horses were killed in a fire on the grounds which sullied her mood a great deal. The king was very quick to replace her horses and gift Margaret with richly-adorned velvet saddles as well.

The royal couple rode into Edinburgh together and were married in person on the 8th of August. While Margaret settled into her new home, her official affairs (and those of England on her behalf) were conducted by the Earl of Surrey, Thomas Howard. Though Margaret was still a young girl, she had become Queen of Scotland and as such did not appreciate her business being conducted by Surrey and his wife. Shortly after the wedding, she wrote to her father to assure him all was well, and could not help alluding to her distaste at being treated like a child.

> Letter from Margaret Tudor, Queen of Scots, to her father, Henry VII
>
> *"My most dear lord and father, in the most humble wise that I can think, I recommend me unto your Grace, beseeching you of your daily blessing, and that it will please you to give hardy thanks to all your servants the which by your*

*commandment have given right good attendance on me at this time. And especially to all these ladies and gentlewomen which hath accompanied me hither, and to give credence to this good lady the bearer hereof, for I have showed her more of my mind than I will write at this time.*

*Sir, I beseech your Grace to be good and gracious lord to Thomas, which was footman to the Queen my mother, whose soul God have pardon; for he hath been one of my footmen hither with as great diligence and labor to his great charge of his own good and true mind. I am not able to recompense him, except the favor of your Grace.*

*Sir, as for news I have none to send, but that my lord of Surrey is in great favor with the King here that he cannot forbear the company of him no time of the day. He and the Bishop of Murray ordereth everything as nigh as they can to the King's pleasure. I pray God it may be for my poor heart's ease in time to come. They call not my Chamberlain to them, which I am sure will speak better for my part than any of them that be of that counsel. And if he speak anything for my cause, my lord of Surrey hath such words unto him that he dare speak no further.*

*God send me comfort to his pleasure, and that I and mine that be left here with me be well entreated such ways as they have taken. For God's sake, Sir, hold me excused that I write not myself to your Grace, for I have no leisure this time, but with a wish I would I were with your Grace now, and many times more, when I would answer.*

*As for this that I have written to your Grace, it is very true, but I pray God I may find it well for my welfare hereafter. No more to your Grace at this time, but our Lord have you in his keeping.*

*Written with the hand of your humble daughter*

*Margaret [sic]"*

Henry VII's treaty of peace lasted for the remainder of his reign, giving his daughter and King James enough time to start their family. As Margaret was only 13 years old at the time of the marriage and not necessarily physically ready to have children, the couple's first child was not born until 1507. Queen Margaret gave birth at least six times but only one of her children reached adulthood: James V, born April 10 1512.

After the death of King Henry VII in 1509, Margaret's younger brother Henry inherited the throne and was not much interested in upholding the diplomatic work accomplished by his father. Almost at once, Henry VIII embarked upon a military campaign in France which clearly overstepped the careful rules of the Treaty of Perpetual Peace that his father had signed with James IV. France and Scotland were long-time allies, so once the new English king stepped foot in France intent upon conquering the nation piecemeal, King James IV was obligated to wage war on England. He did so first by sending ships to France and then by personally leading an attack south of the border to try to capitalize on the English king's absence from his own realm. The plan went terribly wrong and James was killed at the Battle of Flodden, leaving Margaret widowed with a young son at the age of 23. The king's body was collected and embalmed but eventually lost somewhere in England.

James' will designated his wife as regent over their baby son James Stuart but stipulated that she remain a widow. She did so during the following year as she faced detractors who wanted to place John Stuart, her husband's closest relative apart from his son, in her place as regent. Margaret kept her head and negotiated with her adopted countrymen until most of the would-be revolutionaries had lost their sense of urgency. She was at the forefront of a peace pact between Scotland, her brother's kingdom to the south, and France, which was under the rule of Louis XII.

Despite her intelligence and legitimate claim to the Scottish regency, Dowager Queen Margaret found herself alone in a position of power and struggled not to become overwhelmed. She'd been used to ruling at the side of her capable husband, not relying solely on her own counsel in all matters. She sought out a powerful companion, though perhaps not consciously.

The queen's eye fell to Archibald Douglas, a Scottish nobleman born in the same year as she was. Douglas' father had just died alongside King James IV at the Battle of Flodden, and with the death of his grandfather soon afterward, Archibald began the 6th Earl of Angus. His family was an important force within Scottish politics, which is why he came to the attention of the widowed queen. Margaret fell in love rapidly and married Douglas in a secret ceremony on August 6, 1514. When the Scottish nobility and the other members of the royal family found out about the marriage, they were extremely upset.

The first order of business for John Stuart and his supporters was to strip Margaret of her role as regent. She knew this would be a consequence of becoming someone's wife, but what she didn't expect was for the new regency's Privy Council to take away her right to be involved in her children's lives at all. Furious, she took her sons James and Alexander to Stirling Castle with some of their supporters to keep the boys out of the hands of the new regent, Duke of Albany. Douglas ran home to Forfarshire.

It was a move that caused a tug-of-war over the boy king and nearly sparked civil war throughout Scotland. John Stuart knew that his role as regent was useless if he were not in possession of little James V, but he couldn't simply send an army to Stirling and knock down the door, since such a move would endanger the life and wellbeing of the young king. In the summer of 1515, however, the Duke of Albany received both the Stuart children into his custody after Margaret discovered she was pregnant and vulnerable. Her brother, King Henry VIII of England, wrote to her with great concern and begged her to return to his kingdom so he could ensure her safety.

Once the boys were out of her custody, she met with her husband and did just that.

It was August of 1515 when Margaret and Archibald arrived in the north of England. In October of the same year, the Dowager Queen gave birth to a daughter, Margaret Douglas, at Harbottle Castle, Northumberland. A few months after delivering her healthy baby girl, Margaret learned that her youngest son, Alexander, had died under the protection of John Stuart. He was not quite two years of age. Margaret was further entrenched in misery when Archibald left her to return to Scotland and beg the Earl of Albany for forgiveness. He was forgiven and took up with a new woman, the Lady Jane of Traquair. Margaret was down, but not beaten. She remained in England for several years and bided her time, only being allowed to visit with her son once. When her son turned 12, she seized a chance to regain her authority and power.

The Scottish Regent traveled to France in 1524 to oversee his troops' performance in the ongoing Italian Wars. While he was gone, young King James V turned 12 and was considered by many to be of a sufficient age to rule the kingdom without the guidance of a regent. The time was right for Margaret, who re-entered Scotland, met up with her allied families, and took her son from Stirling Palace to Edinburgh. Parliament met in the summer and officially declared James V the undisputed, independent leader of Scotland. A winter Parliament recognized Margaret Tudor Stuart's right to act as an advisor to her royal son. After his deposition by Parliament, the Earl of Albany remained mostly in France.

While the ousted regent backed down peacefully, the Earl of Angus, Margaret's estranged husband, did not. He'd had another daughter with his mistress and forsaken his wife politically. He'd been charged with treason and exiled to France but escaped to England where Margaret's brother eventually allowed him to return to Scotland. Margaret did not respond positively. When Angus attempted to join the Parliament upon his return to his own country, she actually fired cannons in his direction.

Margaret was unable, ultimately, to keep her husband out of parliamentary proceedings, nor was she immediately able to obtain a divorce. Douglas took full advantage of his leeway and kidnapped his step-son James V. Angus kept control of the king for three years, acting as the major power behind the crown until 1528, when the fifteen-year-old king forcibly removed himself from the custody of his self-appointed protector. The same year, Margaret was granted a divorce from the Pope. She married Henry Stuart, another relation to her first husband, and was welcomed back to court by her son.

Once he'd obtained the throne for himself and could act as he saw fit, King James V embraced the advice and nearness of his oft-estranged mother. Probably as a kindness to Margaret, James named her new husband Lord Methven. Together, the family arranged peace once more between Scotland and England by the year 1534. Four years later, King James V married Mary of Guise, a girl who was very friendly with her husband's mother.

There were no more political upheavals during Margaret Tudor's lifetime, though her third husband took up with a mistress and fell very much out of her favor. She was not granted a second divorce, and so continued to reside often at Methven Castle. In 1541 at the age of 41, the Dowager Queen of Scotland died at home at Methven. She was interred at the Perth Charterhouse. Her son had been summoned shortly before her death but arrived too late to make his farewells. He had his mother's belongings packed up from her husband's house and delivered to his own residence.

Margaret's only other surviving child was Margaret Douglas, who lived a long life and enjoyed a close relationship with her uncle Henry VIII. She married Matthew Stuart, 4th Earl of Lennox and was grandmother to King James VI of Scotland, eventual inheritor of the English realm from Queen Elizabeth I.

# Chapter 9 – Mary Tudor, Queen of France

Mary Tudor was the youngest surviving child of King Henry VII and Elizabeth of York. Born on March 18, 1596, she was brought up in her own household, which was traditional for all royal children of the era. From the age of six, Princess Mary had her own household of servants, educators and advisors. She was taught embroidery, Latin, French, music, and dancing like her sister Margaret.

From a young age, Mary was considered a beautiful and talented girl – which for a princess meant that she could be easily used in political strategies between kingdoms. An early engagement to Charles of Castile was canceled in lieu of a peace treaty crafted by her brother's advisor, Cardinal Wolsey. She didn't have long to wait before Henry and his council found their ideal use for her as the third wife to the elderly French King Louis XII. France and England were in a constant state of rivalry, particularly over Calais and many other regions on the continent that had changed hands between them more than a few times. A marital match between the French and English crowns stood to accomplish much for both parties.

King Henry VIII's little sister was 18 years old when she set out to France to marry King Louis, a match 34 years her senior. She was accompanied across the English Channel by Lady Joan Guildford and four younger ladies-in-waiting, one of whom was Mary Boleyn. Once the party reached Paris, Mary's retinue was joined by Anne

Boleyn. On the 9<sup>th</sup> of October 1514, Mary Tudor married King Louis XII at Abbeville before moving with her new husband to the court at Paris. She'd already had a proxy wedding at her brother's palace in England, as was tradition. There had been a lavish party in August of 1514, two months before the couple met face to face. The royals and their guests had a wonderful time, Mary dressed in her finest new clothes, and the French Duc de Longueville acted as proxy for his king. The two even climbed into a bed together so Longueville could touch Mary with his unclothed leg – simulating marital consummation.

At 52 years of age, King Louis had no living sons and still harbored hopes that he may yet beget a son with his young English wife. When Louis died three months after the wedding, the French court laughed that he must have overdone himself in the marital bed, though given his age and ongoing battle with gout, it was more likely the latter that ended his life. Whatever the reason for Louis' death, it signaled freedom and relief for Mary, now Dowager Queen of France.

Before the young girl could go home to England, however, she had to wait and see if she'd become pregnant with an heir to France. At the bidding of Francis I, cousin to the deceased king, Mary stayed in isolation for six weeks to determine whether or not Louis had impregnated her. When it was clear she was not growing a French heir in her womb, Francis I officially took over the throne of France and Mary was cleared to leave.

In England, Henry VIII sent one of his closest friends, the newly-created Duke of Suffolk (Charles Brandon), to collect his sister and bring her home. It was a risky move since Henry knew full well that Mary was in love with Brandon, but the king trusted the latter not to make anything of it. The King made Brandon promise not to be charmed by Mary and urged him simply to ensure her safety on the voyage back to England. Suffolk promised and set off to do as he was bid.

Henry and Charles had a particularly special friendship because they had spent part of their childhoods in the same household. At the Battle of Bosworth, at which Henry VII had defeated Richard III and taken the English throne, it was Brandon's father who had borne the Tudor standard. William Brandon was killed during the battle, so the first Tudor king had Brandon's son Charles educated with his own children. As adults, Henry and Charles had a very familial and trusting relationship. It was for exactly this reason Brandon was entrusted with the most delicate and personal of tasks on the part of Henry VIII.

When Mary's traveling companion arrived in France, Francis I had questions about the future of the Dowager Queen of his country. The French king wondered what the future would hold for this girl who was still very young and politically valuable. He wanted to know if she required another marriage within France, and if so how he could help. There were discussions of perhaps arranging a wedding between Mary and Antoine, Duke of Lorraine, or Charles III, Duke of Savoy.

Mary did indeed have marriage in mind, but it was to no one in France or on the continent. She told Francis that she wanted to marry Charles Brandon and said she would be very grateful for his blessing in doing so. Since the French king saw no reason such a marriage shouldn't go forward, he made all the arrangements. Charles, for his part, was surprised at how far his secret betrothal had gone without him knowing a thing about it. Mary was adamant, however, and she knew very well that he'd married his first two wives solely for ambitious purposes. Her instincts were good, since Charles could surely do no better than an English princess and a French queen. More than that, the two had a history together thanks to Henry VII and were probably very comfortable with one another. Worse marriages had been arranged without the knowledge of one of the parties.

Though Mary wrote to her brother asking for his blessing, Henry didn't have time to respond in the negative before she and Charles went through with the wedding. It took place on March 3, 1515, in the presence of King Francis I and only nine other witnesses.

King Henry was not amused. At a time when the nobility required the permission of the king to marry, it was incredibly disobedient and insulting of his sister and friend to do such a thing. Whether he approved of the match or not, Henry was an egotistical king who certainly resented not having been consulted properly.

He wrote angry letters to both his sister and the Duke of Suffolk, remonstrating them for moving so quickly in a foreign land and without so much as his knowledge, let alone his consent. His sister wrote back, reminding Henry that he had promised her she could marry whomever she pleased after the old French king died. She appealed to his brotherly love and asked forgiveness.

Letter from Mary Queen-Dowager of France to Henry VIII:

*"My most dear and entirely beloved brother,*

*In most humble manner, I recommend me to your grace.*

*Dearest brother, I doubt not but that you have in your good remembrance that whereas for the good of peace and for the furtherance of your affairs you moved me to marry with my lord and late husband, King Louis of France, whose soul God pardon. Though I understood that he was very aged and sickly, yet for advancement of the said peace and for the furtherance of your causes. I was contented to conform myself to your said motion, so that if I should fortune to survive the said late king I might have affixed and clearly determined myself to marry with him; and the same [I] assure you hath proceeded only of mine own mind, without any request or labour of my said lord Suffolk, or of any other person. And to be plain with your grace, I have so bound myself unto him that for no cause earthly I will or may vary or change from the same. Wherefore my good and most kind brother, I now beseech your grace to take this matter in good part, and to give unto me and to my said lord of Suffolk your good will herein. Ascertaining you, that upon the trust and comfort which I have, for that you have always honourably regarded your promise, I am now come out of the realm of France, and have put myself within your jurisdiction in this your town of Calais, where I intend to remain till such time as I shall have answer from you of your good and loving mind herein; which I would not have done but upon the faithful trust that I have in your said promise. Humbly beseeching your grace, for the great and tender love which ever hath been and shall be between you and me, to bear your gracious mind and show yourself to be agreeable thereunto, and to certify me by your most loving letters of the same till which time I will make mine abode here, and no farther enter your realm. And to the intent it may please you the rather to condescend to this my most hearty desire, I am contended and expressly promise and bind me to you, by these presents, to give you all the whole dote which delivered with me, and also all such plate of gold and jewels as I shall have of my said late husband's. Over and besides this I shall, rather than fail, give you as much yearly part of my dower, to as great a sum as shall stand with your will and pleasure; and of all the premises I promise, upon knowledge of your good mind, to make unto you sufficient bonds. Trusting, verily, that in fulfilling of your said promise to me made, you will show your brotherly love, affection, and good mind to me in this behalf, which to hear of I abide with most desire; and not to be miscontented with my said lord of Suffolk, whom of mine inward good mind and affection to him I have in manner enforced to be agreeable to the same, without any request by him made; as knoweth our Lord, whom I beseech to have your grace in his merciful governance. [sic]"*

Charles Brandon also wrote to his friend, the king, apologetically. He had no particular excuses and simply stated that he knew he'd upset Henry but that he didn't truly expect much to come of it. His overconfidence in his friend probably didn't help the situation, because the newly-married couple decided to stay in Calais until Henry's mood lightened.

Technically, Charles Brandon had committed treason by marrying a royal princess without the king's consent. There were those among the king's council who wanted him to be put to death, or at least imprisoned. Henry decided to fine the couple. He charged them an astonishing 24,000 pounds for their recklessness, confiscated the 200,000-pound dowry Mary had received from King Louis XII and took all the traditional marriage gifts Mary had received from the French king. In Mary's letter, she handed the money and plates – a customary marriage gift, for fine dining sets were expensive – over to her brother happily.

The costs of the fine itself were insurmountable. Henry agreed to let Mary and Charles pay 1000 pounds per year for their rights to return to his court and continue on in their privileged lives as before. Of course, Mary and Charles agreed, however even wealthy nobles could not afford such annual payments. After the first part of the debts were paid, a second wedding was arranged at Greenwich Palace in the presence of King Henry VIII and his courtiers. The English ceremony took place on May 13, 1515, after which both the bride and the groom were soon back in the good graces of King Henry.

Mary Tudor was Brandon's third wife, so upon their marriage she became stepmother to two girls named Anne and Mary. She spent most of her time with the girls and her own children at Westhorpe Hall in Suffolk, though Brandon was often in London at court with Henry. The couple had two daughters, Francis and Eleanor, and a son named for his father.

Though she was referred to as the French Queen for the rest of her life, Mary Tudor Brandon lived the life of a Duchess of Suffolk. She raised her children, cared for the household and attended important events at her brother's court from time to time. Having already been acquainted with Mary and Anne Boleyn when the sisters had attended her in France, Henry's sister had developed a strong disliking of Anne that resurfaced in the 1530s. As King Henry distanced himself permanently from Queen Catherine of Aragon and attempted to make Anne Boleyn his wife, Mary spoke out against her brother's mistress. There was only so much displeasure and anger she could allow herself, however, since Henry had graciously lowered her debts and was responsible for her financial wellbeing.

In 1528, Mary contracted the sweating sickness, a little-understood disease of the time. The symptoms of the illness came on rapidly in its victims, beginning with the feeling of cold, shivering, and light-headedness. After an hour or so of cold, those infected began to sweat heavily and suddenly. An oppressive feeling of heat then followed, as well as thirst, headache and delirium. Often, victims of the sweating sickness died within hours of the first symptoms. If they survived, they had not gained immunity, since people could contract the same illness again and again.

Mary survived her ordeal but was never fully healthy afterward. It has been theorized that perhaps the Duchess of Suffolk suffered from a form of cancer or heart disease that was exacerbated by her bout with the sweating sickness. Six months after her brother married Anne Boleyn, Mary died at her home in Suffolk.

The French Queen was beloved by many and her death resonated throughout England and France. At her funeral, a French delegation attended to offer their condolences. Both her biological and step-children jostled for position behind her casket as it made its way to the abbey. Mary's was interred at Bury St. Edmonds Abbey in Surrey, then later moved to St. Mary's Church when Henry had the monasteries dissolved. Since custom forbade a monarch or a grieving spouse to attend a funeral, neither Charles nor Henry were present at her final ceremony.

Her children were integral to the future of the royal court – particularly Frances Brandon. She was born on July 16, 1517, in Hertfordshire but she spent the bulk of her childhood at the Brandon home in Suffolk. Unlike many children of noble parents, Frances and her siblings were raised together in the same household as their mother. All the Brandon children received a good education just as their father and mother had at the pleasure of King Henry VII. Frances visited her uncle Henry's court in London regularly and became very fond of Queen Catherine of Aragon. She met her cousin Mary there and developed a friendship that would be lifelong. Frances married into the Grey family and was mother to de facto Queen of England, Jane Grey.

# Chapter 10 – The Birth of the Church of England

Despite her military victory, Catherine continued to fail in her most essential task as queen: producing a male heir. Henry VIII respected his wife and trusted her completely, but he was not satisfied with only a daughter as an heir. Henry was adamant that he needed a son to inherit the throne of England. The Wars of the Roses ultimately stemmed from the question of whether the line of succession could pass through female descendants; Henry VIII wanted no such ambiguity to cripple the Tudors. The king grew desperate for sons.

When the king's daughter, Princess Mary Tudor, was nine years old and her mother was 40, King Henry fell in love with his wife's lady-in-waiting. Her name was Anne Boleyn, and she was of the noble birth required to serve at court. The king wrote numerous letters to Anne and sent her extravagant gifts of jewelry. Anne, however, was well aware that Henry had multiple mistresses at court – included her own sister, Mary. Anne refused the king's gifts and advances, asserting her belief that no happiness would come to her in the role of mistress:

> "*If you ... give yourself up, heart, body and soul to me ...*" wrote Henry, "*I will take you for my only mistress, rejecting from thought and affection all others save yourself, to serve only you.*"

To which Anne replied: *"Your wife I cannot be, both in respect of mine own unworthiness, and also because you have a queen already. Your mistress I will not be."*

Henry was not a man used to being told *no*, and soon became determined to secure Anne Boleyn for himself. The devoutly Catholic king found permission to discard Catherine of Aragon and marry the woman he loved passionately in an unlikely source: the Book of Leviticus.

*"And if a man shall take his brother's wife, it is an unclean thing: he hath uncovered his brother's nakedness; they shall be childless."*

Whether Henry genuinely believed that his lack of sons was God's punishment for his marriage to Arthur's widow, or whether his thorough study of the Bible had rewarded him with the perfect excuse to exercise his lust, the king began to consult his councilors and spiritual advisors on the matter.

Divorce was initially out of the question for a Catholic king, not to mention completely unprecedented for a royal couple in the 16th century. When Henry convinced his lawyers and the Archbishop Thomas Cranmer that he intended to remarry, whatever the consequences, they decided the best course of action was to seek an annulment on the basis that Queen Catherine had consummated her previous marriage to Arthur Tudor.

Popes were not in the habit of granting annulments to adult couples who had a child together. The courts struggled with the king's mandate for six years, waiting for approval from the Catholic Church that never arrived. Henry had promised Anne Boleyn they would marry as soon as it was legally possible, but with no permission from the Church forthcoming, Henry and Anne wed in a secret ceremony in November of 1532. The marriage was legalized in a second wedding the following January. In May of 1533, Archbishop Cranmer presided over a special court that rendered null and void the king's marriage to Catherine and certified his new marriage to Anne as valid—without the approval or consent of Pope Clement VII.

Catherine of Aragon was beyond insulted and humiliated at the public display her husband made of dissolving their marriage. Catherine had fought fiercely against the annulment proceedings, insisting that she and Arthur had never consummated their marriage. She had the Catholic Church on her side, as well as the support of her family in Spain. In the end, neither was sufficient to change Henry's mind.

In 1535, Henry had Catherine taken to Kimbolton Castle in Cambridgeshire. She was deeply depressed and never conceded to Henry's wish that she no longer call herself the Queen of England. His jilted first wife locked herself in her own rooms at the castle, only leaving to attend Catholic mass and meet with visitors.

One precious visitor who was not permitted to see Catherine was her daughter Mary. Henry repeatedly asked mother and daughter to recognize Anne Boleyn as their queen in exchange for visitation rights, but they both refused. Mary was incredibly loyal to her mother, and both women were staunch Catholics. They could not conscientiously bow to Anne, nor could they disobey the orders of the pope, now Paul III, who had excommunicated Henry. Friends of the former queen and her daughter smuggled letters between the two, but at court they had both fallen out of favor.

Catherine of Aragon died on January 7, 1536, after a long period of constant fasting and self-deprivation. On the day she was buried as a Dowager Princess of Wales at Peterborough Cathedral, Henry did not attend the service, and forbade his daughter Mary to pay this last respect to her mother.

Henry VIII's decision to go forward with the marriage to Anne Boleyn, despite the explicit instructions from the Pope not to do so, caused a split between him and the Catholic Church. In 1532, after waiting years for word from the Church on his proposed marriage to Anne, Henry had reached a breaking point. On the king's behalf,

Henry's chief minister Thomas Cromwell drafted the Statue in Restraint of Appeals. The Act, passed in April of 1533, made the king the final authority in England on all matters, including religious questions—and made it illegal to accept the authority of the pope. In November 1534, Parliament passed the First Act of Supremacy, which proclaimed Henry the Head of the Church of England. Henry's kingdom had become a Protestant nation.

The signs of this religious reformation became quickly visible throughout England. Ornate churches were robbed of their gargoyles, angels, and other Catholic symbols, and monasteries were knocked down. Statues of the saints were removed from their pedestals, many of which remain empty half a millennium later. New printing presses shared the stories of the Bible for everyone to read – whereas Catholics were expected to hear the Bible only as interpreted by their priest.

Henry VIII, in his insistence to marry his wife's lady-in-waiting, ended up changing his entire kingdom for centuries to come. He was fiercely proud of this fact, and took seriously his responsibility to educate his people on matters of religion.

To the confused ranks of religious leaders during the Reformation, Henry said:

> *"Alas, how can the poor souls live in concord when you preachers sow amongst them in your sermons debate and discord? They look to you for light and you bring them darkness. Amend these crimes, I exhort you, and set forth God's word truly, both by true preaching and giving a good example, or else, I, whom God has appointed his vicar and high minister here, will see these divisions extinct, and these enormities corrected."*

Henry VIII may have gotten his way in his battle with the Church, but he had not yet gotten his son. On September 7, 1533, Anne Boleyn gave birth to Elizabeth Tudor, much to Henry's disappointment. After Elizabeth's birth, Anne, like Catherine before her, endured several miscarriages. On the same day Catherine of Aragon was buried, the now-unquestioned Queen Anne delivered her last baby—a stillborn boy. Her misfortune would only increase.

# Chapter 11 – King Henry VIII: Wives Two and Three

Henry VIII was considered a very handsome and athletic king when he began his reign. He was quite tall for the time period—probably above six feet in height—and he was an avid sportsman. Henry enjoyed hunting on horseback and jousting with his courtiers and knights. The Henry VIII who married Anne Boleyn was a man who truly seemed to have it all. His physique in later years was a stark contrast to this original image. In fact, when he died, the king could only be described as obese and ill; he was suffering from several chronic medical problems. One of these ongoing ailments was ulcerated legs, an injury generally attributed to a jousting accident at the age of 44, mere months before Henry ultimately lost his temper with the new queen.

A contemporary witness to the scene wrote about what he saw on the mock battlefield:

> *"On the eve of the Conversion of St. Paul, the King being mounted on a great horse to run at the lists, both fell so heavily that everyone thought it a miracle he was not killed, but he sustained no injury. Thinks he might ask of fortune for what greater misfortune he is reserved, like the other tyrant who escaped from the fall of the house, in which all the rest were smothered, and soon after died."*

Both jousters crashed at the pinnacle of the match and fell heavily to the ground. Despite the commenter's assertion that he was uninjured, Henry suffered a serious head injury. He was reported "unable to speak for two hours."

It was by no means the first time Henry had suffered an injury from his favorite sport, and in all other cases Henry had healed and recovered his health in full. His accident in 1536 was different. In time, Henry was well enough again to speak and work, but he never joined in a jousting competition again. His accident is thought by many historians and medical researchers to have marked an important transition between the first and second parts of Henry's life. Whereas before the accident the king was athletic, confident and boastful, afterward he was considered sullen and considerably less sporting in nature. In particular, some believe that the king's temper would never quite recover.

Anne's final miscarriage occurred in the days following Henry's accident. Despite the fact that his wife was still quite young and healthy, Henry was not content to keep waiting. Fewer than three years after the most controversial marriage in English history, the king once more sought to remarry.

Henry's second annulment was politically simpler than the first, but just as emotionally draining. Anne was constantly furious with her husband for his affairs with various ladies at court,. He excused himself by blaming her for their continued lack of a male heir. When their relationship was too volatile to continue, Henry called in his advisors and lawyers.

The king's prime advisor, Thomas Cromwell, was all too happy to find a new wife for his monarch. Cromwell did not have a good relationship with the Boleyn family and he was eager chance to do away with an enemy while simultaneously pleasing the king. To speed along the annulment, Anne was imprisoned and put on trial for several charges. These included adultery, high treason and incest – the latter based on the claim that she'd had an improper relationship with her own brother. Historians believe that the king's allies falsified most, if not all, of the charges brought against Anne.

Found guilty, Anne's marriage was annulled and she was sentenced to die. Her brother, George Boleyn, shared the same sentence and was executed two days before Anne. The final victim of the charges against the queen was William Brereton, a servant to the king. Brereton was found guilty of committing adultery with Anne. He died on the same day as George.

At the executioner's block, Anne was serene and calm. Prepared for death, she spoke to the people gathered before her.

> *"Good Christian people, I am come hither to die, for according to the law, and by the law I am judged to die, and therefore I will speak nothing against it. I am come hither to accuse no man, nor to speak anything of that, whereof I am accused and condemned to die, but I pray God save the king and send him long to reign over you, for a gentler nor a more merciful prince was there never: and to me he was ever a good, a gentle and sovereign lord. And if any person will meddle of my cause, I require them to judge the best. And thus I take my leave of the world and of you all, and I heartily desire you all to pray for me. O Lord have mercy on me, to God I commend my soul."*

It is impossible to say whether the king's head injury truly did change his character, but we do know that mere months after his fall, Henry had Anne Boleyn - the wife for whom he changed all of England - imprisoned, denounced as queen and executed. He would continue to acquire and discard wives in quick succession, never truly content with any of them—with the exception of his third wife, Jane.Anne Boleyn was executed on Tower Hill on May 19, 1536. Less than a fortnight later, Henry VIII married Jane Seymour, former lady-in-waiting to both Queen Catherine and Queen Anne. Jane was seven years younger than Boleyn and remarkably different than the king's first two wives.

Jane Seymour also came from a good family but had not received the extensive education that her predecessors had. She was not an avid reader or writer, like Catherine and Anne, and is said only to have been able to read and write her own name. She enjoyed more traditional homemaking skills such as embroidery and gardening. Known generally as a sweet and mild-mannered young woman, Jane nevertheless had strong conservative views concerning the way her household should be run. She banned her serving ladies from wearing the vibrant French dresses that had been so popular with Anne Boleyn and other young women at the time.

Jane was the opposite of Catherine and Anne, which is quite possibly what enticed Henry VIII to her in the first place. He was a boisterous and confident king who, at that point in his rule, desired very little input from his spouse. He wanted a woman who was happy in herself, and content to know her place within his life and palaces. For her part, Jane was perfectly aware of the fate that met Henry's first and second queens, and would have thought very carefully before speaking out against her powerful husband.

There were, however, two matters for which she sought Henry's ear. A few months into his third marriage, Henry faced the first major internal challenge to his break with the Catholic Church. Unhappy with the king's suppression of the Catholic church, a group of nobles organized what became known as the Pilgrimage of Grace. Led by Robert Aske of London, the Pilgrimage gathered the support of some 40,000 people in the north of England. The pilgrims marched to Lincolnshire Church and occupied it in the name of their Catholic rights. They continued onward to Doncaster, where they were met by lords from nearby counties who represented the king. Seeing the great number of people, Henry's representatives decided to talk with Robert Aske and see if the two parties could come up with a peaceful solution to the Catholics' grievances. When the Duke of Norfolk, Thomas Howard, told Aske that the king would grant the people a parliament, Aske accepted this proposal and told his followers that they should be grateful.

Henry VIII, of course, had not been consulted, and was not at all willing to hold any such parliament with the Catholic faction. Jane Seymour appealed to her husband for leniency, but Henry ignored her defenses of Aske and his pilgrims. After several more forays between Aske and the king's men, the leader of the pilgrimage was executed, as were thousands upon thousands of his followers. It was an unprecedentedly ruthless move on the part of the king, but as he saw it, protecting the Church of England was vital. He would no longer deal with any talk against his reformation of England.

Jane Seymour had more success with a second matter: the status of Henry's two daughters, Mary and Elizabeth. Queen Jane, as she was known despite her lack of official coronation, held family in the highest regard. For this reason, she wanted her husband to accept his young daughters back into his life, as much for his own emotional and spiritual welfare as for theirs. Because Mary and Elizabeth had been made illegitimate upon the annulments of their respective mothers, they were no longer part of the royal household, nor were they considered potential heirs to the throne of England. Jane hoped to restore the girls to their rightful titles. In particular, she bonded with Mary and felt deep sympathy for the plight of Queen Catherine. Her sympathy for Catherine, and for Robert Aske's pilgrims, suggests that Jane may have been a Catholic sympathizer, though this potential private leaning was never revealed to the public.

On October 12, 1537, Queen Jane gave birth to Edward Tudor. The baby boy was healthy and strong – the first of Henry's sons to thrive. It was the biggest achievement of Queen Jane's short life. While Edward endured his elaborate christening ceremony, Jane became very sick. Over the next twelve days, she experienced a high fever and bouts of delirium. She craved sweets and wine, both of which were provided for her, but there was nothing to save her life. Jane Seymour died on October 24.

King Henry VIII was genuinely pained by the death of his third wife. He wore mourning clothes of deep black for over three months following Jane's burial, and even took up her quiet hobby of embroidery to keep her pensive, calm ways in memory. Most surprisingly, Henry waited two full years before marrying again.

# Chapter 12 – King Henry VIII: The Last Three Wives

When the mourning period was emotionally past and Henry found time once more to desire a woman at his side, the king's advisors and friends made haste to procure one to his liking.

Anne of Cleves was selected for her noble status and her nationality. Born in Dusseldorf, then part of the Holy Roman Empire, Anne of Cleves came from a family that had also rejected the rule of the pope. Thanks to Henry's Reformation, England had a strained relationship with most countries in Europe, and the king wanted to forge new bonds outside of his own realm. With both Anne and her younger sister, Amalia, under consideration to become his next wife, Henry sent his court portraitist to visit the Cleves household and create true likenesses of the women on canvas.

The artist, Hans Holbein the Younger, had the difficult task of creating a very quick portrait that would be sent back to Henry and his advisors. Art historians have suggested that Holbein had already marked up much of the canvas before the actual portrait sitting, meaning that the women's features were quite generic. Whatever the exact process, Holbein sent back his completed portraits on time. King Henry VIII was happy with the picture of Anne and decided to move forward with the marriage contract.

Shortly before the wedding, Anne traveled to England to take up residence in London. Excited to meet her, Henry arrived in costume so that he might playfully tease the lady before unmasking himself and revealing his true identity. Upon seeing her for the first time, the king rushed back to his advisor, Thomas Cromwell, and shouted "I like her not!" Unfortunately, though Anne of Cleves had many genuine admirers of her beauty, Henry was not one of them. Anne was quite tall and broad-boned, with a large nose. Though these features were well-blended given her frame, the king had simply envisioned a smaller woman from the portrait he'd studied.

Henry met with Anne before the wedding ceremony took place, when there was still time to back out of the marriage. For unknown reasons, he chose to move forward with the wedding despite his misgivings at Anne's physical features. Perhaps he placed a great deal of importance on his reputation in the rest of Europe; perhaps he decided to see if, in time, he would grow to appreciate the young woman.

Anne was only 25 years old when she married the 48-year-old Henry VIII. There was very little to attract a man like Henry to young Anne, since she was not as well-educated or as dainty and small as his former wives and lovers. Nevertheless, the two were married on January 6, 1540.

Whatever made Henry go forward with the wedding was not enough motivation to actually consummate the marriage. After his first night with Anne, Henry confessed to his manservants they he had put his hands all over the new queen in an attempt to become aroused, but it was to no avail. Confused about just what constituted marital consummation, Anne wrote happily to her mother, claiming that she was happy in the marriage and everything was going as it should.

King Henry would never spend the night with Anne of Cleves. Instead, true to form, he decided to have the marriage annulled so that he could marry one of her ladies-in-waiting. By July of 1540, just six months after their wedding, Henry VIII and Anne of Cleves had their marriage declared illegal and illegitimate. The jilted bride was neither executed nor cast out of the royal houses, however. In a rare show of empathy and respect, King Henry declared that henceforth, Anne of Cleves was his "sister" and the owner of several beautiful, rich estates throughout the kingdom. She was given a luxurious annual salary from the crown and lived the rest of her life a rich woman in England. She died in 1557 at the age of 41.

On the July 28, 1540 – the very same year in which Henry had married and divorced Anne of Cleves – the king married his fifth wife: Catherine Howard. She was merely a teenaged girl at the time of the wedding, estimated at 16 or 17 years of age. Henry was nearly 50.

The king was delighted at the youth and vivacity of little Catherine Howard. Catherine enjoyed dance lessons and could read and write, but was otherwise quite uneducated. The fifth Queen of England by Henry VIII's side had been raised at the large estate house of her father's step-mother, the Dowager Duchess of Norfolk, but her upbringing there was somewhat controversial.

At the estate of the Dowager Duchess, many young girls from noble families were in the care of the lady of house. This was a common practice at the time, intended to help the girls learn aristocratic manners while saving their families money on their upbringing. The Dowager Duchess was not particularly strict with respect to how the girls spent their spare time. Given free reign, Catherine and her roommates had a habit of letting neighborhood boys into their sleeping area at night. Much worse, however, was Catherine's experiences with her music teacher, Henry Maddox. Catherine would later admit that, from the age of 13, Maddox had molested her at the Duchess' estate.

At the age of 15, Catherine had begun a long-term romance with an employee of her patroness: Francis Dereham. According to sources close to the Catherine, she and Francis had a sexual relationship and referred to one another and "wife" and "husband." When the

Dowager Duchess discovered the young couple's relationship, she sent Dereham away to Ireland.

The very young queen was, therefore, both experienced in the sensual parts of life and accustomed to the control of powerful—and brutal—men. Upon the teenager's marriage, King Henry VIII must have seemed just as much an imposition to her small self as had Henry Maddox. The king was no longer the attractive royal catch he had once been. He was around 300 pounds and quite sick most of the time. At nearly 50, the once-slim and attractive young king had grown unrecognizably fat, soft and rather intolerant. In the wake of his jousting accident, perhaps the king had taken solace in two pleasures that were left to him; food and drink. His body had expanded rapidly over the course of his rule, adding up to 20 inches of girth around his chest. As the same time, he grew less patient with his wives, less empathetic with his advisors and less merciful towards the people of England and Ireland. At this point in his life, women most likely feared telling him "no."

The relationship between Catherine Howard and King Henry VIII was brief. While living at the palace, she soon fell in love with one of the king's servants, Thomas Culpeper, and the two of them began an affair. Queen Catherine was not a practiced writer and must have taken a great deal of time to form each word in the following letter to Thomas Culpeper:

> *"I never longed so much for a thing as I do to see you and to speak with you, the which I trust shall be shortly now. That which doth comfortly me very much when I think of it, and when I think again that you shall depart from me again it makes my heart die to think what fortune I have that I cannot be always in your company."*

The king's staff uncovered letters between Catherine and Culpeper, and Henry had Catherine imprisoned in the winter of 1541. Thomas Culpeper and Francis Dereham, Catherine's former lover, were found guilty of high treason and executed that December.

Catherine's sentencing came late in January, after Parliament created a brand-new law by which she would retroactively be found guilty of treason. On February 13, 1542, Catherine Howard was helped up the steps to the executioner's scaffold and decapitated. Her body was disposed of in the same mass grave as her cousins, Anne and George Boleyn. King Henry VIII did not attend the execution.

Henry VIII's final choice for queen was Katherine Parr. She was 31, twice-widowed and childless—a complete turnaround from Howard. With Parr, there was no chance to accidentally assume her virginity and find her lacking; there was no reason to expect children that would never come. At 51, Henry's legs were covered in very painful boils that had to be regularly lanced by his doctor. Because of his size and pain, he could barely move around the Palace of Whitehall. The reason for his marriage to Katherine Parr at such a difficult point in his life was actually quite pure and simple: Henry VIII wanted female companionship from an experienced woman he could trust. The two married on July 12, 1543, at Hampton Court Palace.

Mary, Elizabeth and Edward were all in attendance and would receive much positive attention from their new stepmother. When she became the Queen of England, Katherine Parr had already seen two husbands grow sick and die; she must have known that this particular bout of nursing and caring for a sick man would come to an end soon enough.

Katherine had been raised in the rural north of England and knew little about the exciting life of courtiers and kings, but she was an educated woman who never stopped learning. When she moved to Henry's palace as his sixth queen, Katherine was pleased to join in the frequent philosophical and spiritual discussions of the day. She was a devout Reformer, and as she learned more on the subject of religion, she made sure that Henry's children learned alongside her. In particular, she took on the education of Elizabeth and Edward, creating perhaps the most well-educated noblewoman England had ever seen. The two future monarchs became stoic Protestants, due in no small part to Katherine's guidance.

Unfortunately, some of the Catholic advisors at court believed that the queen went too far in her constant Protestant campaign. They convinced Henry that she was perceived as an evangelical and a heretic. The king arranged for a contingent of guards to arrest his wife the next day, but also had a courtier slip the arrest warrant under Katherine's door to warn her. The queen rushed immediately to her husband's rooms and spoke with him, assuring him that she deferred to him in all matters, including theological ones. He smiled and seemed pleased with her.

The next day, however, the arresting officials returned. They approached the royal couple while Katherine, ever a gentle and caring wife, sat beside the king and massaged his swollen legs. Lord Wriothesley announced that he had come to arrest Queen Katherine and take her away.

Katherine must have struggled to hold on to her senses – after all, two wives before her had been mercilessly killed for displeasing the king. But Henry VIII knew very well that many of his advisors and courtiers sought to use his characteristic anger and swift judgment for their own purposes. He had orchestrated the entire incident to demonstrate to his court that he was the master of his own mind. When the guards came to arrest his queen, he physically struck them and sent them all away humiliated. Katherine was safe under Henry's protection.

Parr remained a dutiful wife to Henry VIII until his death in 1547 at the age of 55. Henry spent his last days suffering greatly in bed. His infected boils stank and none of his courtiers or attendants dared tell him the end was near, since Henry himself had enacted a law that forbade anyone to speak of the death of a monarch.

Modern medical professionals have speculated that the king suffered a variety of illnesses, including diabetes and syphilis. These could explain his ulcers, night sweats, extreme thirst and mental degradation in the last few years of life. Another potential culprit, a neurological disorder known as McLeod's syndrome, could account for the rapid change in Henry's health and demeanor starting in 1536, as well as the repeated miscarriages and stillborn births suffered by his many wives.

King Henry VIII died on January 28, 1547. He was not yet 56 years old. He was interred beside Jane Seymour, the woman he claimed was his one true wife.

Katherine Parr's relationship with her royal stepchildren continued long after the king was gone, as she remained their most eager tutor. A few short months after becoming a royal widow, Katherine married for a fourth time to Thomas Seymour, the brother of Henry's beloved Queen Jane. She loved him deeply but died in childbirth the following year.

Anne of Cleves outlived both Henry VIII and his other five wives. She stayed at Hever Castle on her ex-husband's generous allowance for nearly two decades, a frequent and beloved guest at the English court. She died in 1557 at the age of 41.

# Chapter 13 – King Edward VI

Henry VIII called little Prince Edward the kingdom's "most precious jewel." He gave his prized son all the toys and comforts he could ever want, and provided him with a thorough education in European languages, philosophy and religion. Despite the romantic entanglements of his father, Edward enjoyed the sort of family life that his own father had. He spent holidays with Katherine Parr, Henry VIII and his sisters, Mary and Elizabeth. In 1546, the family spent their first Christmas together thanks to the persuasion of Queen Katherine. At that time, Henry officially claimed both daughters as legitimate and welcomed them as part of the Tudor family. Each of Henry's children was henceforth an heir to the throne of England.

The siblings were all close, but Edward preferred the company of Mary the most. He had a bit of a rivalry with Elizabeth, who was a spectacular student in the siblings' combined lessons. Edward was also credited with great intelligence; his main interests were finance and military history and strategy.

Young Edward had a relatively healthy childhood. Hoping to protect his sole male heir from disease, the king ensured that his son's rooms were scrupulously cleaned. Like most children, Edward contracted several illnesses during his childhood, including a form of malaria. Overall, however, he was considered a vivacious and fast-growing boy.

As was tradition, Edward Tudor was the subject of various marital schemes by his father and other royal families throughout Europe. Since Henry VIII wanted to unite Scotland and England, he decided that the best course of action was to marry young Edward to Mary, the infant queen of Scotland. Mary was only six days old when her father, King James V, died. He had no other legitimate heirs. With Scotland under the power of various regents, Henry VIII saw an opportunity. The Treaty of Greenwich, signed in 1543, promised that the six-month-old Mary would marry Edward, then age five, upon reaching her tenth birthday. Part of the treaty included the stipulation that Mary be sent to the English court to be raised as Henry VIII saw fit.

Ultimately, Scotland reneged on its agreement and instead made a new contract with its old ally, France. Mary was to be sent to the French court for her education and eventual marriage to the Dauphin Francis, heir to the French throne. Edward's father was outraged. In retaliation, and in the hope that the Scots might respond to more heavy-handed persuasion, he ordered Edward Seymour—brother to Jane Seymour and uncle to Edward—to lead an invasion of Scotland. The fighting lasted from 1543 to 1551, and later became known as the "Rough Wooing." Though Scotland sustained horrible losses at the hands of Seymour's forces, it refused to marry off its little queen to the English.

Before Henry VIII died, he stipulated in his will that, should Edward inherit the throne before the age of eighteen, a party of sixteen personally-selected executors would share the power of the crown. In the final weeks and days of Henry's life, the will was amended so that the old king's wishes were less clear. Upon Henry's death in 1547, his son was crowned King Edward VI in a short ceremony befitting a child. Afterward, though Henry's intended executors did take power, state affairs were almost wholly handled by Edward Seymour. Seymour named himself Lord Protector of the Realm and

Governor of the King's Person. It was not the Regency Council that the old king wished for, but Edward was too young to understand such matters or make corrections. Until the age of fifteen, King Edward VI watched a never-ending power struggle between relatives and council members.

At first, Seymour's war against Scotland gave him great respect at court and established him as the king's main regent. Soon, however, popular opinion collapsed into revolts across England. The people were angry that further Protestant measures—fully supported by the Edward, the first English king to be raised a Protestant—were being imposed in their churches. Particularly egregious was the translation of the Bible into English. The kingdom-wide distribution of the first England-language liturgical text, called Book of Common Prayer, enraged Catholics as well as conservative Protestants. Both groups believed that Latin was the ideal translation for their holy texts, and were angry at the fact that now the Bible could be read and interpreted—or, worse, misinterpreted—by any literate English person.

Only two years into Edward's reign, his uncle Edward Seymour was overthrown from his position in the Regency Council charged with various crimes against the crown, including ambition, reckless war and stealing from the royal treasury. The ambitious John Dudley replaced Seymour as head of the council. With his uncle in prison, Edward VI happily deferred to Dudley in matters of state. In fact, entries in his personal journal portray Edward VI as quite emotionally detached from his authoritative uncle and most other members of the Regency Council. When Seymour, sensing that his time as Lord Protector of the Realm was nearing an end, fled to Windsor with the young king, Edward wrote in his journal: "Me thinks I am a prisoner." A later entry proclaimed, with little sympathy, "The Duke of Somerset had his head cut off upon Tower Hill between eight and nine o'clock in the morning."

In his teenage years, Edward VI grew into a potent and opinionated king, though he could not yet rule independently: "I will say with certain intention, that I will see my laws strictly obeyed, and those who break them shall be watched and denounced." Edward was dedicated to the new regime his father had established and enacted several measures to increase the influence of the Church of England. These included government-appointed church ministers, rights of the clergy to marry, and communion for common people. Clergy who outright disapproved of the reformations of the church – such as the Bishops of Winchester and London - were imprisoned in the Tower of London.

Most of the work of officiating church reform fell to Edward's chief advisor, the Archbishop of Canterbury Thomas Cranmer, who had also served Henry VIII. The Archbishop wrote extensively in order to clarify the reformation laws. One of the most important of these documents was the Forty-two Articles, in which Cranmer outlined the Church of England's stance on various religious questions. For example, Cranmer explained that, while traditional Catholics believed that the bread and wine taken at communion were literal pieces of Jesus Christ's body, members of the reformed religion should treat the reference to Christ's body as merely symbolic. These and other highly-contested issues of the time needed clarification from King Edward so that clergy, commoners and law-keepers understood how to perform their roles and avoid punishment.

In 1553, when Edward VI was fifteen years old, he fell ill with tuberculosis and did not recover. Fearing the worst, he decided to choose his potential successor rather than leave the kingdom to his half-sister Mary. Though Mary had already been declared heir after Edward by Henry VIII, the 37-year old Catholic was not the ideal candidate for a newly-Protestant kingdom. The obvious choice for Edward seemed to be his Protestant sister Elizabeth, but the teenage king surprised everyone by picking his first cousin, Jane Grey.

Jane Grey was the great-niece of Henry VIII by way of his younger sister, Mary Tudor. She had been raised in the household of Katherine Parr, often joining her cousins Edward and Elizabeth for their studies. But it was not merely Jane's devoutness and her relationship with Edward that inspired the young king chose his cousin to succeed him. Jane's father-in-law was none other than John Dudley, Edward's chief advisor. The wording of the dying king's succession document was jumbled, but tell-tale signs of corrections were present. The line "Lady Jane heirs male" had been changed to "Lady Jane *and her* heirs male," which meant that Jane herself, not only any male offspring, was part of the line of succession.

The last words of King Edward VI were recorded for posterity:

*"I am faint; Lord have mercy upon me and take my spirit."*

Four days after Edward's death on July 6, 1553, Lady Jane Grey was proclaimed Queen. She never made it to her coronation.

# Chapter 14 – The Nine Days' Queen, Jane Grey

Born the same year as Edward, Lady Jane was a teenage newlywed when she ascended to the throne. Though she did indeed possess royal Tudor blood, she was never groomed for the crown, nor did she at any point in her life – including during Edward's illness – expect to become Queen. However, her father-in-law, John Dudley, was all too eager to pave the way for her, and he was perfectly positioned to do so as Edward VI's self-proclaimed regent.

Upon Edward VI's death, any successor to Edward VI needed to trace his or her lineage back to Henry VII, the first Tudor king—and there was a strong preference for candidates who were male. There were, however, no male Tudors available. A quick look backwards through the royal family tree proved that there were only two other candidates for the throne beside Henry VIII's own two daughters.

Henry VII had produced four children: Arthur, Henry VIII, Mary and Margaret. Arthur died before he could become a father; Edward Tudor was Henry VIII's only son. Mary Tudor's eldest child was daughter Frances Grey, whose eldest child was daughter Jane Grey. Margaret Tudor had married King James IV of Scotland. Of their six children, only James V survived into adulthood. James V's only living child was Mary Stuart.

Mary Stuart was an unlikely choice. This was the same Mary whom Scotland had promised, and then denied, to five-year-old Edward as a future bride. Now ten years old, Mary was living in the court of the French king, where she would one day be married to his son. Furthermore, her uncle Henry VIII's will had excluded Mary, and the entire Stuart line, from succession. If, as many argued, both Mary and Elizabeth were illegitimate by virtue of Henry VIII's annulments, and if Mary Stuart had been eliminated by Henry VIII's last will and testament, then Jane Grey was the only possible heir to the throne. John Dudley, Jane's powerful father-in-law, arranged to have her Jane Grey taken to the palace and sworn in as Queen.

While Edward lay on his deathbed, Mary was at home in Hunsdon, Hertfordshire. When the king died, she was making preparations to visit her half-brother at his request. Before she could make the journey, she received an important warning from a friend. Mary was told that Edward VI wanted to entrap her and have her imprisoned, so that once he was dead she could not raise an army against Jane. It was the ultimate insult to Mary, who had been very close to her brother in his early youth.

Mary took this warning to heart and fled instead to East Anglia, where she did indeed put together an army. There were many Catholics in East Anglia, and they supported her with horses and armed men. She wrote immediately to Edward's Privy Council and made it clear that she intended to take what she believed was rightfully hers. Henry VIII's eldest daughter had such strong numbers behind her that riots broke out in London. In the name of Queen Mary, Queen Jane was captured and deposed only nine days after she had been brought to the palace. Mary had not even arrived in the capital before her enemy was charged with treason and imprisoned in the Tower of London.

Crowds cheered as Mary Tudor rode into London on August 3, 1553, alongside her half-sister Elizabeth. More than 800 members of the nobility marched with her. There was no more question of the validity of Mary's rule. Mary was a strong woman who knew her mind; Jane, twenty years her junior, was girl afraid of causing trouble. Nevertheless, the Nine Days' Queen, as she came to be known, had proven herself a threat to be contained. Jane, her husband Guildford Dudley, her father-in-law John Dudley, and her own father were all arrested and imprisoned at the Tower.

During her imprisonment, Jane wrote to her cousin Mary in an attempt to explain herself.

> *"Although my fault be such that but for the goodness and clemency of the Queen, I can have no hope of finding pardon.... having given ear to those who at the time appeared not only to myself, but also to the great part of this realm to be wise and now have manifested themselves to the contrary, not only to my and their great detriment, but with common disgrace and blame of all, they having with shameful boldness made to blamable and dishonourable an attempt to give to others that which was not theirs...[and my own] lack of prudence...for which I deserve heavy punishment...it being known that the error imputed to me has not been altogether caused by myself. [The Privy Council] ....who with unwontd caresses and pleasantness, did me such reverence as was not at all suitable to my state. He [Dudley] then said that his Majesty had well weighed an Act of Parliament...that whoever should acknowledge the most serene Mary...or the lady Elizabeth and receive them as the true heirs of the crown of England should be had all for traitors...wherefore, in no manner did he wish that they should be heirs of him and of that crown, he being able in every way to disinherit them. And therefore, before his death, he gave order to the Council, that for the honour they owed to him...they should obey his last will...As to the rest, for my part, I know not what the Council had determined to do, but I know for certain that twice during this time, poison was given to me, first in the house of the Duchess of Northumberland and afterwards here*

*in the Tower.... All these I have wished for the witness of my*
*innocence and the disburdening of my conscience. [sic]"*

With Jane Grey and John Dudley locked up, Mary turned her
attention to the Catholic Bishops who had been locked in the Tower
for nearly the entirety of her brother's rule. Thomas Howard and
Stephen Gardiner were immediately released and given new titles.
Gardiner was restored to Bishop of Winchester and created Lord
Chancellor. He crowned his redeemer Queen Mary I on October 1,
1553 at Westminster Abby. The next month, Jane and her fellow
prisoners were put on trial. They were found guilty and sentenced to
death.

On February 12, 1554, Jane was beheaded at the Tower of London.
Before her death, she addressed the crowd assembled below the
scaffold:

> *"Good people, I am come hether to die, and by a lawe I am*
> *condemnded to the same. The facte, in dede, against the*
> *quenes highnesse was unlawfull, and the consenting*
> *thereunto by me: but touching the procurement and desire*
> *therof bt me or on my halfe, I doo wash my hands thereof in*
> *innocencie, before God, and in the face of you, good*
> *Christian people, this day."*

Jane tied a handkerchief around her eyes, laid her head on the block,
and echoed the last words of Jesus on the cross:

> *"Lorde, into thy hands I commende my spirite! [sic]"*

# Chapter 15 – Queen Mary Tudor I

Mary was a powerful mixture of her parents; She was ruthless like Henry VIII and faithfully Catholic like Catherine of Aragon. Though she had publicly forgiven her father for keeping her away from her mother in final years of Catherine's life, Mary had never accepted that England was a Protestant kingdom. To Mary, there was only one thing she must do during her reign: reunite with the Catholic church. This plan had been growing in her mind since she and her mother were forced out of Henry VIII's court. A letter from Catherine of Aragon at that time urged Mary to do as her father said and avoid causing problems, for her own sake and safety:

> *"Daughter,*
>
> *I heard such tidings today that I do perceive (if it be true) the time is very near when Almighty God will prove you; and I am very glad of it for I trust he doth handle you with a good love. I beseech you, agree of His pleasure with a merry heart; and be sure that, without fail, He will not suffer you to perish if you beware to offend Him. I pray you, good daughter, to offer yourself to Him...And if this lady [Shelton] do come to you as is spoken, if she do bring you a letter from the King, I am sure in the self same letter you shall be commanded what you shall do. Answer with few words, obeying the King, your father, in everything, save only that you will not offend God and lose your own soul; and go no further with learning and disputation in the matter. And wheresoever, and in*

*whatsoever, company you shall come, observe the King's commandments.*

*But one thing I especially desire you, for the love that you do owe unto God and unto me, to keep your heart with a chaste mind, and your body from all ill and wanton company, [not] thinking or desiring any husband for Christ's passion; neither determine yourself to any manner of living till this troublesome time be past. For I dare make sure that you shall see a very good end, and better than you can desire...And now you shall begin, and by likelihood I shall follow. I set not a rush by it; for when they have done the uttermost they can, then I am sure of the amendment...we never come to the kingdom of Heaven but by troubles. Daughter wheresoever you come, take no pain to send unto me, for if I may, I will send to you,*

*Your loving mother,*

*Katherine the Queen [sic]"*

After years of letting herself be pushed around by King Henry and his advisors of the reformed church, Mary had no remaining patience left for her tenure as queen. Though she superficially accepted England's dual nature with reference to religion, she truly believed that Catholicism was the one true faith. Alone, Mary could do little to reinstate Catholicism in her country, so she sought an ally abroad. Philip II fit the role perfectly, and he came recommended by his father, King of Spain.

Born in 1527, Spain's heir to the throne of Catholicism's most faithful nation was eleven years younger than Mary. Still, the match made sense to England's new queen, who undoubtedly wanted to reconnect with her mother's Spanish side of the family. The marriage was arranged quickly, much to the pleasure of Mary, who was both enamored with Philip and very eager to become pregnant. She was 37 years old but hopeful that she could produce an heir of her own. If she did not, upon her death the kingdom would fall into the hands of her Reformist half-sister, Elizabeth. Her anxiety over that potentiality drove her to imprison Elizabeth in the Tower of London.

When she discovered her fate, Princess Elizabeth wrote promptly to her half-sister:

> *"March 16, 1554.*
>
> *If any ever did try this old saying, 'that a king's word was more than another man's oath,' I most humbly beseech your Majesty to verify it to me, and to remember your last promise and my last demand, that I be not condemned without answer and due proof, which it seems that I now am; for without cause proved, I am by your council from you commanded to go to the Tower, a place more wanted for a false traitor than a true subject, which though I know I desire it not, yet in the face of all this realm it appears proved...*
>
> *And as for the copy of the letter sent to the French King, I pray God confound me eternally if ever I sent him word, message, token, or letter, by any means, and to this truth I will stand in till my death.*
>
> *Your Highness's most faithful subject, that hath been from the beginning, and will be to my end,*
>
> *ELIZABETH,*
>
> *I humbly crave but only one word of answer from yourself."*

To ensure that his son Philip would be named King of England, Charles V of Spain gave his son the kingship of Naples and Jerusalem before the proposed wedding. Mary ensured that her husband would be called King of England, with his name beside her own on all royal documents. The couple was married on July 25, 1554 at Winchester Castle.

Mary's court was afraid that under the kingship of a Spaniard, England would lose its independence. This fear was exacerbated when the queen showed classic signs of pregnancy. At her advanced age, many expected her to die in childbirth, and a document was drawn up by Parliament declaring King Philip the Regent of England upon Mary's death. Impervious to the dangers and gossip, Queen Mary was excited and full of joy with her Catholic husband from Spain and a baby on the way. She was happy and comfortable enough to have Elizabeth released from prison. Unfortunately, her projected due date for the baby's delivery came and went. Several months after the false rumor that she had given birth to a boy, Queen Mary's pregnancy symptoms disappeared. There was no baby.

Soon afterwards, King Philip II departed his wife's side to attend to matters in the Netherlands, then a part of the Spanish Empire. Mary was devastated. Lonely and depressed, she blamed her failure to conceive and give birth on her having been too accepting of the rampant Protestantism of her country. She became more fixated than ever on eliminating from England those she deemed heretics. It was this moment in Mary Tudor's life that changed her into the infamous Bloody Mary of legend.

Desperate to make up for her self-perceived sins against the Catholic Church, Mary orchestrated her own version of her grandparents' Spanish Inquisition. Queen Mary and Pope Julius spent several months negotiating England's return to the Catholic realm. Under the restoration agreement, anti-heresy laws were passed and Protestants were rounded up and burned at the stake en masse. It was both reminiscent of the rule of Ferdinand and Isabella of Spain, who ruthlessly prosecuted Jews and Muslims in their kingdom, and of Henry VIII's punishment of the anti-Protestant protestors in the north of England. Mary was ruthless and became feared throughout the country.

Thomas Cranmer, the Archbishop of Canterbury and Edward VI's most trusted religious advisor, was an immediate and obvious target for Queen Mary. As England's most powerful member of the Church of England, aside from the monarch, Cranmer had created new rules, doctrine and biblical interpretations that infuriated Mary and the Catholic Church. Mary made the Archbishop watch his colleagues being burned alive. Cranmer agreed to become a Catholic after being tortured, but his words were not enough for the queen. She ordered him to be burned at the stake on March 21, 1556. Before the fire consumed his body, Cranmer confirmed his belief in the Protestant Reformation.

King Philip II returned to England in 1557 to ask for his wife's help protecting the Holy Roman Empire, of which his father had been emperor, from the conquest of France. She agreed, despite contrary advice from her council. Severe flooding in England had caused meager harvests and very few resources; the costs associated with sending troops to the continent further depleted the country's treasury. Although English and Spanish troops successfully guarded Spain's authority in Italy, England lost its last piece of land in France: Calais.

Queen Mary suffered one more false pregnancy before becoming very sick – possibly from a uterine disease – and dying on November 17, 1558. During her five-year reign, she had an estimated 300 people burned alive.

# Chapter 16 – Elizabeth Tudor

Mary's crown fell directly to the last remaining child of King Henry VIII: Elizabeth Tudor. No longer imprisoned by her sister, Elizabeth was living in Hatfield, Hertfordshire, when Mary's condition degenerated drastically. Upon Mary's death, she came directly to London and was immediately pronounced Queen of England.

England was in sorry shape when Elizabeth was crowned on January 15, 1559. Queen Mary's death ended a chaotic and violent reign that earned her the nickname "Bloody Mary." The quick succession of four monarchs in the relatively short time since King Henry VIII's death was reminiscent of the flurry preceding Henry VII's rule. Once again, the people craved the kind of stability in the monarchy that would enable peace and prosperity. Elizabeth needed to address the financial crisis and a food shortage in addition to the intense distrust between Catholics and Protestants in the kingdom.

Elizabeth's first obstacle was her gender. That her predecessor was also a queen may have been a disadvantage to Elizabeth, as Mary was considered an over-emotional ruler. Though only 25 at her coronation, Queen Elizabeth was an intelligent woman and she fully intended to prove herself:

> *"As for my own part I care not for death, for all men are mortal; and though I be a woman yet I have as good a courage answerable to my place as ever my father had. I am your anointed Queen. I will never be by violence constrained*

*to do anything. I thank God I am indeed endowed with such qualities that if I were turned out of the realm in my petticoat I were able to live in any place in Christendom."*

The Protestants who had endured five years of persecution under Mary were less concerned about the queen's gender; they were desperate to feel safe and free to worship in their own way. When Elizabeth quickly declared that England was to be a Protestant kingdom again, they rejoiced. The country and the international community remembered that Elizabeth was the child of Anne Boleyn, the very woman for whom Henry VIII had broken with the pope and established the Church of England. For Protestants, this fact bolstered their appreciation for the new ruler and gave them hope for the future of their country. After years of unprecedented persecution, the reign of terror had come to an end for the die-hard members of Henry VIII's religion.

Elizabeth's decision to reinstate the Reformation was celebrated by half her people, but the other half feared for their lives in this world and their souls in the next. She had a lot of work to do to allay the fears of everyday Catholics, and to subdue the most radical Catholics who would challenge her reign. Most Catholics agreed that the burning of supposed heretics needed to stop, and were willing to make some concessions to the Protestants in order to live peacefully. When Elizabeth canceled her sister's re-association with the pope, the decision was expected and not fiercely contended. The queen tried to blend some elements of traditional Catholicism into the Church of England's rulebook, including vestments for the clergy and the use of crucifixes. This more moderate approach to religion offended many, but it was not so strict so as to cause immediate revolt or backlash. Elizabeth required her parliament and advisors to swear an oath of allegiance to herself as the Supreme Governor of the Church of England, but she also did away with heresy laws so that anyone who refused would not face torture and death.

Elizabeth's panel of advisors—many of whom had served her brother Edward as well as her sister Mary—were primarily concerned with two things: whether Catholic Europe would invade the island, and who the young queen would choose as a husband. At first, Elizabeth graciously played hostess to an onslaught of potential suitors from home and abroad. Mary's widower, King Philip II, was happy to continue on as England's king beside Elizabeth instead of Mary, but Queen Elizabeth refused his proposal. Furthermore, since Spain remained devoutly Catholic, the arrangement between the two countries no longer made sense. Proposals followed from kings and princes of Austria, France and Sweden. Elizabeth, considered flirtatious and very much entertained by the endless line of suitors, kept most of her suitors guessing, often for years. It became clear very soon into her reign that Queen Elizabeth was already in love with an Englishman and therefore unlikely to marry anyone else. Unfortunately, the object of her affection was already married.

Robert Dudley, the queen's childhood friend and apparent love interest, was the son of John Dudley, the man who had orchestrated Jane Grey's ascension to the throne. Robert Dudley had rallied troops for Jane before she was stripped of her crown, and as a consequence was sent to the Tower of London alongside his father and brother. Coincidentally, Elizabeth was imprisoned at the same time by her sister. Both were released and eventually restored their family's titles and lands.

Robert had served King Edward VI, most auspiciously by helping the king's army crush the Catholic rebellion of 1549. By the time Elizabeth Tudor became the Queen of England, she and Robert had known each other for many years. According to courtiers, the two often flirted publicly and were suspected of being in love with one another. Of course, though the Council and Parliament were eager for their queen to find a husband, Dudley's wife, Amy Robsart, stood in the way of such a match.

Rumors were rampant at Elizabeth's court that she was waiting for Dudley's wife—apparently very ill—to die so that she could marry Robert. As the years wore on and the queen still refused all marriage proposals, her suitors generally believed this rumor to be true. In

1560, when Amy Robsart died after a fall down the stairs, many believed that Robert or even the queen herself had arranged for the woman's murder. Aware of such gossip and concerned about how a wedding would reflect on them, the couple never did marry.

In 1562, the queen contracted smallpox. Without a husband, a child or even a chosen heir, Elizabeth's government worried that the country would succumb to civil war upon her death. It was very telling that on her sickbed, Queen Elizabeth hastily chose someone as Protectorate of the Realm: Robert Dudley. This decision was never acted upon, however, since the 29-year-old queen was nursed back to health.

Much of the work of caring for Elizabeth during her long days of sickness fell to her friend and lady-in-waiting, Mary Sidney. Unfortunately, Mary herself fell victim to the same disease while she played nursemaid. She also survived but was terribly disfigured. Her husband wrote of the ravages of smallpox on his wife:

> *"When I went to Newhaven [Le Havre] I lefte her a full faire Ladye in myne eye at least the fayerest, and when I retorned I found her as fowle a ladie as the smale pox could make her, which she did take by contynuall attendance of her majesties most precious person (sicke of the same disease) the skarres of which (to her resolute discomforte) ever syns hath don and doth remayne in her face, so as she lyveth solitairilie sicut Nicticorax in domicilio suo [like a night-raven in the house] more to my charge then if we had boorded together as we did before that evill accident happened.[sic]"*

Though Elizabeth was not terribly scarred by her ordeal, the illness had left her with marks. She took to wearing heavy white lead makeup after her recovery, as well as a wig that may have covered small patches of baldness from scarring.

During the beginning of Elizabeth's rule, her cousin Mary Stuart was in France while regents and councils ruled Scotland. Following the death of Mary's husband, the French king, the Queen of Scots finally returned to the country of her birth.

During her reign, Queen Elizabeth saw the formation of a country that had truly moved out of the Middle Ages. England's first theatre was built by Richard Burbage; William Shakespeare wrote plays and performed at the queen's palaces. Francis Drake navigated the world's oceans and explored North America in the name of England. England's armies defeated the Spanish Armada in 1588 and 1597. She chose never to marry, but instead to carry the burden of the monarchy alone. She was proud and defensive of her position:

> *"[F]rom my years of understanding ... I happily chose this kind of life in which I yet live which I assure you for my own part hath hitherto best contented myself and I trust hath been most acceptable to God. From the which if either ambition of high estate offered to me in marriage by the pleasure and appointment of my prince ... or if the eschewing of the danger of my enemies or the avoiding of the peril of death ... could have drawn or dissuaded me from this kind of life, I had not now remained in this estate wherein you see me. But so constant have I always continued in this determination ... yet is it most true that at this day I stand free from any other meaning that either I have had in times past or have at this present."*

Queen Elizabeth of the House of Tudor reigned England and Ireland for over 44 years, a time which is looked upon as the Golden Age. Her era was not just defined by political strategy, strife with Scotland, France and Spain, and an onslaught of royal suitors. Though the mid-16$^{th}$ century was largely defined by poor harvests, war with Ireland, a population boom of around one million people, and an increase in poverty, the last part of the century brought better tidings. For the first time, the whole of Ireland came under English control. Harvests and economies improved, lessening the suffering of the common people so that they might enjoy some leisure time at the theater or pub.

The first theaters were built throughout the kingdom when Elizabeth was on the throne, and due to her love of plays she kept them open despite an outcry from clergy who believed actors, costumes, drama, and stories all posed a threat to the immortal soul. It was even suggested that the black plague, which swept through English cities every summer, was sent by God as punishment for acting in or watching plays. The queen found this preposterous and continued to attend the theater. Many of her courtiers became patrons of the arts, commissioning plays, books, and poetry by the likes of William Shakespeare and Christopher Marlowe.

William Shakespeare arrived in England during the early part of the 17th century and wrote many plays that were performed for the queen herself. Theater was just the start of the entertainment and arts renaissance, however. While the poor and rich gathered together in playhouses, writers and university students resided side-by-side in London's inns and boarding houses. It was an explosive environment in which the artistic minds of so many influential people flourished and developed. Nicolas Hilliard created fine portraits in miniature form, silver jewelry became vogue among England's growing upper middle class, and architects designed manor houses for the nobility based on classical Greek styles and modern Dutch patterns.

The arts thrived thanks to a stable and strengthening economy within England and Ireland. Elizabeth enacted several laws that had a positive impact on the local economy, including several referred to as the "poor laws." The poor laws affected homeless and disabled people, as well as those who were out of work. In a general sense, Elizabeth made vagrancy illegal, but she also wrote legislation that told her local Justices of the Peace what to do with a vagrant. The disabled, aged, or underaged homeless, for example, were cared for in the newly-established almshouses. The Justices of the Peace were allowed to collect taxes in their towns to fund the almshouses and provide the most basic care for anyone housed within them. Anyone deemed fit to work was employed in whatever labor force was available, though treatment of such workers was by no means what modern laws would consider humane.

With more people at work, England's primary fabric-weaving industry held strong, but there were more products incoming from the New World. Elizabeth had commissioned Francis Drake and Walter Raleigh to sail to the American continents throughout the latter 1500s, and there they claimed lands in her name, bringing back gold, tobacco, potatoes, tomatoes, and other valuable goods. Merchants during this time frame had much to celebrate and the industry boomed as English people discovered a love of tobacco. Though vegetables from the New World were less popular and often considered poisonous, they eventually caught on and revolutionized British agriculture and cuisine.

Queen Elizabeth also attempted to boost the economy by requiring individuals to work in the same area in which they were born – this was intended to stop poor farmers and tradespeople from flocking to the city in search of work, and thereby keeping food production up. She also fixed wages, but this was less than effective since food prices kept rising. Despite ongoing difficulties in helping the people earn enough money to care for themselves, Elizabeth did manage to pay down the considerable debts amassed by her father and other royal predecessors.

Elizabeth never did marry, for which reason she was sometimes referred to as the Virgin Queen. She proclaimed herself "married to England," and when pressured about the problem of the succession after her death, she avoided answering or changed the subject. As the last child of Henry VIII, without an heir of her own, Elizabeth's crown would have to go to another branch of the royal family. Her two Tudor aunts had passed away, leaving only Margaret Douglas or James VI of Scotland the most probably contenders.

At the beginning of the 17th century, an aging Queen Elizabeth retired to Richmond Palace on the River Thames and mourned the loss of many of her close friends and servants. Her health deteriorated quickly, beginning with depression. The coronation ring she had not removed since it was placed upon her finger in 1558 was forcibly removed after having grown into her finger – some believe this caused an infection that led to sepsis. Ladies-in-waiting on the queen reported that she either could not or would not sit down, standing for as many as fifteen hours a day before collapsing onto piles of cushions on the floor. One serving lady even reported that Elizabeth suffered visions of ghosts who gave her guilt – including Mary, Queen of Scots and Katherine Grey, sister of Nine Days' Queen Jane Grey. At the end, she lost the ability to speak or stand from the floor. Her ladies arranged her on the bed and councilors visited, paying their respects as well as looking for her answer to the succession.

When James VI's name was mentioned, Elizabeth apparently signified her desire for him to act as her heir by circling her head with a finger to indicate a crown. She died aged 69 years on March 24, 1603 and the honor of filling her place on the throne of England fell the King of Scotland. It was the first time one monarch ruled over both kingdoms.

Queen Elizabeth's body was sealed in a lead coffin with her likeness carved on the cover, then driven by barge on the Thames to Westminster Abbey. The coffin was pulled through the streets of London on a horse-drawn hearse before its permanent interment at Westminster. She shares her tomb with her half-sister, Queen Mary I.

# Chapter 17– Mary Stuart, Queen of Scots

Queen Elizabeth's main rival during her reign was her cousin Mary Stuart, the child of the English queen's cousin Margaret Douglas and King James V of Scotland. Mary was born in December 8, 1542, just six days before her father died from a sudden illness. She inherited the Scottish throne upon James' death and the Duke of Arran, James Hamilton, became her main regent. Almost immediately, the royal infant received two serious marriage proposals from England and France.

The first proposal came from King Henry VIII, who wanted to match Mary to his son, Prince Edward. Arran informally agreed to this proposal on behalf of his ward, but broke his promise soon afterward. The second proposal came from King Henry II of France, who wanted Mary to wed his own son, Francis. As France and Scotland were long-standing allies, Arran ultimately decided to accept the French offer and forsake Henry VIII. To cement the deal, Mary herself was sent to France in 1550 to be raised at the side of her future husband. In Mary's absence, her mother Mary of Guise ruled Scotland as regent, having put aside Arran in 1544.

Mary Stuart stayed in France with her future in-laws for 13 years and completed her education there as part of the inner circle of the French court. Her father-in-law was kind and fatherly to her, but apparently Mary's mother-in-law, Catherine de Medici, had a disliking for the girl. The royal children married in 1558 and became King and Queen of France in 1559 after Henry II died in a jousting accident. Mary was 16 years old and Francis II was 15. Only 17 months later, Francis died from complications from an ear infection and left Mary Dowager Queen and a widow. The same year, Mary's mother died in Scotland. Nine months after the death of Francis, Mary Stuart returned to Scotland.

She was 18 years old, Dowager Queen of France, ostensibly next in line to the throne of England, and active Queen of Scotland. Mary was the most powerful woman in Europe, but she lacked political prowess. She also lacked familial support, since the Tudor queen was suspicious of her, and the unfriendly Catherine de Medici ruled France as regent for Francis' younger brother Charles IX. At home, there was violence and derision between Catholics and Protestants that was inflamed by Mary's staunch Catholicism. Hers was not an easy transition from one kingdom to the other.

She had not been in Scotland since she was a very small child and was unsure of the local customs and culture. Further, she was a devout Catholic arriving to a small kingdom of Catholics and Protestants who were constantly at arms with one another. She was the rightful Queen of Scotland, but she felt powerless and out of place. In 1565, Mary married her cousin, Henry Stuart, the Lord Darnley, hoping to solidify her position. Mary's southern neighbor, Queen Elizabeth Tudor, was immediately apprehensive.

Not only had English King Henry VIII purposefully overlooked the Stuarts for the line of succession, but Mary had been raised and educated in an enemy nation as far as he was concerned. In marrying Henry Stuart, the Scottish queen was essentially pairing her Tudor blood with that of another distant Tudor; Elizabeth was not impressed. She knew well enough how easy it could be for relations of the crown to find supporters and build an army; if the Catholics among her own people were unhappy enough they might well join the ranks in support of Mary.

Upon her return to Scotland, Mary's life became rather chaotic. She'd likely hoped that the marriage to another Stuart would solidify her authority and give her the emotional and political support of her wider family, but that wasn't what happened. Instead, Mary's half-brother James Stuart, Earl of Moray, saw his chance to make a play for the crown. James Stuart was also a child of the late King James V, but his mother was a mistress of the king. Nevertheless, he had designs on the throne and once Mary wed Henry, he knew how to proceed: By joining the Protestant rebels and giving them a figurehead to rally behind.

Moray raised troops, as did Mary; the armies both set out in the summer of 1565 but neither accomplished much of anything as they did not meet head-on. Finally, in October, Moray set down his arms and fled to England. Queen Mary immediately sought to strengthen her Privy Council by bringing in popular members of the Protestant nobility. Eventually, Moray was allowed to join them.

Mary's husband was a jealous and ambitious man who only added to the queen's problems. First, he insisted that he be crowned equal to her and be given the right to succeed her as Scotland's only monarch if she predeceased him. Second, he believed she was having an affair with her private secretary, the Italian David Rizzio. In the first case, Mary refused. In the second, Henry conspired with friends and murdered Rizzio in plain sight of the queen.

Mary gave birth to another James Stuart in June of 1566, and near the end of that year she had a secret meeting with her most trusted advisors to discuss how to remove her husband from court. In February of the next year, he was found murdered. James Hepburn was accused of the murder by the slain Lord Darnley's father, and under pressure to punish the killer, Mary held a trial for Hepburn. He was acquitted. What happened next has never been properly explained.

Hepburn gathered officials and documented support from many members of the nobility to pursue marriage with the queen. In April of 1567, Hepburn either kidnapped Mary or convinced her to accompany him to Dunbar Castle, where they remained for several days. When they married each other mere weeks later in a Protestant ceremony, the queen's advisors and subjects alike were baffled. The marriage put everyone at odds and led to Mary's forced abdication of the Scottish throne. Her son, James VI, merely an infant, was named king and placed under the care of a regent.

Mary Stuart escaped prison and fled Scotland, seeking the help of her cousin Queen Elizabeth of England and Ireland. Hepburn was exiled from Scotland and eventually died in a Danish prison. Under the guise of compliance, Elizabeth had Mary sequestered at Bolton Castle in Wensleydale and ordered an investigation into the Scottish queen's conduct north of the border. A court hearing was set up to determine whether Mary was guilty or complicit in the death of Henry Stuart. Elizabeth would not allow Mary to attend, but the latter refused outright anyhow. The deposed queen believed that as a foreign monarch she was not subject to the courts of any nation other than her own.

During the hearing, a set of letters were shown as evidence against the Scottish queen. These were not signed, but they seemed to be in Mary's handwriting and they were interpreted as love letters between the queen and James Hepburn. The letters were considered very uncertain proof of Mary's involvement in the death of Scotland's king, and yet they were a very real threat to her. At a Conference between Scotland's Regent, James Stuart, and Elizabeth, the English court declared as their queen wished: Nothing had been proven for or against Mary Stuart. The Regent returned to rule Scotland and Mary remained in English custody.

Queen Elizabeth was simply unsure how to deal with Mary, and therefore left her to languish in Tutbury Castle. The location of Mary's house arrest was very strategically planned to keep her far from the Scottish border and away from the sea. Contained in the middle of England, Queen Mary could not be easily freed by her supporters back home. Mary was well provided for, with a staff of at least 16 ladies-in-waiting and a personal chef. She merely was not allowed to leave the estate.

In 1587, Elizabeth ordered her royal cousin to be executed following her spy's discovery of a plot to replace herself with Mary on the throne of England. By the time of her death, the Scottish queen had been kept in England for 20 years.

# Chapter 18 – King James I and the Tudor Legacy

James Stuart was born on June 19, 1566, and he inherited the Scottish crown as the infant son of Mary, Queen of Scots. Though court portraits show James posed next to his royal mother, the boy was less than a year old when he last saw Mary Stuart. He was twenty years old when she was executed for treason against Queen Elizabeth – rather ironic given that he would eventually inherit Elizabeth's kingdom upon her death in 1603.

The succession of James of Scotland to the English throne was a momentous occasion and it would be the basis for the eventual formation of the United Kingdom of Great Britain and Northern Ireland.

Though technically under the rule of James I, England's Tudor Dynasty came to an end, the monarchy after James were still closely related to the Stuarts, Tudors and even the Plantagenets. In fact, Great Britain's current monarch, from the House of Windsor, is directly descended from King Henry VII and can trace familial roots all the way back to that servant of the Welsh Kingdom of Gwynedd, Ednyfed Fychan. Still, the Tudors are considered a stand-alone epoch of English history.

Under the leadership of Henry VII and his descendants, England changed its religious identity, developed its colonial identity and became Europe's financial center. Henry VIII invested in the Royal Navy and the predecessor to the Royal Mail, while his daughter Elizabeth granted the creation of the Royal Exchange. Ships sailed around the world and brought colonists – as well as the religiously persecuted – to the Americas. Explorers brought back tomatoes, squash and potatoes, the latter of which would eventually become a new superfood in the Old World. Merchants and stockbrokers gathered in London to borrow, lend and invest money. The English fashion industry blossomed, influencing everyone from the future Queen of France to emigrant Puritans. Slowly, over more than a century of Tudor rule, England became more unified, more stable and more self-aware of its place in the world.

Of the dynasty's founder, King Henry VII, the historian Henry Bertram Chrimes said:

> *"If it be true that England showed a greatness and a marked flowering of her spirit and genius in the course of the sixteenth century, such a development would have been inconceivable without the intermediation of Henry of Richmond's regime. Not for him were the vast egoisms of his son Henry nor the gloriations of his granddaughter Elizabeth. But without his unspectacular statecraft their creative achievements would have had no roots."*

It is true that England was forever changed because of the actions of the first Henry Tudor, but historians often overlook the roles played by the women of the family, particularly those who married into the House of Tudor. Without the dedication, commitment, support and personal risks of women like Catherine of Valois and Margaret Beaufort, the magnificent story of Henry Tudor versus Richard III at Bosworth Field may never have existed. If the Tudors hadn't seized the throne, England may have fallen into permanent civil war and the dissolution of the monarchy altogether.

It is easy to see the many ways this powerful and authoritative family changed the world, because of so many things they left behind. The Church of England is not only the largest religion in Great Britain, but Anglicism has spread throughout the Americas as well. Law and order, public support for the poor and even medicine have developed into finely-tuned programs thanks to Queen Elizabeth and King Henry VIII, the latter of whom legalized human dissection and funded public education.

Even the arts blossomed during the Tudor era thanks to the country's stability and growth. No longer constantly focused on internal war, the middle and upper classes of English people discovered talents and appreciation of architecture, paintings, theater and literature. Still today, the plays, poetry, artworks, sculpture and buildings are considered things of great intelligence and beauty.

Truly, the Tudors gave England the strong foundation upon which many great things were – and are still being – achieved.

# Here's another book by Captivating History that we think you'd be interested in

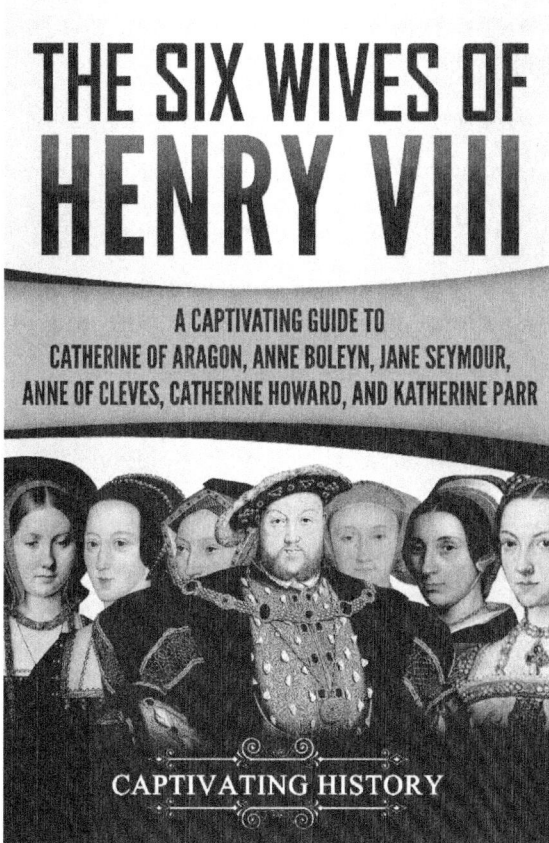

## THE SIX WIVES OF HENRY VIII

### A CAPTIVATING GUIDE TO CATHERINE OF ARAGON, ANNE BOLEYN, JANE SEYMOUR, ANNE OF CLEVES, CATHERINE HOWARD, AND KATHERINE PARR

CAPTIVATING HISTORY

# References

Brady, Ciaran (ed.) *A Viceroy's Vindication? Sir Henry Sidney's Memoir of Service in Ireland, 1556-78.*

*Brigden, Susan (2000). New Worlds, Lost Worlds: The Rule of the Tudors, 1485–1603. London: Allen Lane/Penguin.*

Cheetham, Anthony (1995). *The Life and Times of Richard III.* Head of Zeus.

Chrimes, Bertram Henry (1972). *Henry VII.* University of California Press.

Gairdner, James (1876). *The Historical Collections of a Citizen of London in the Fifteenth Century.* Camden Society.

Hanson, Marilee. *"Queen Catherine Howard to Master Thomas Culpeper,"* https://englishhistory.net/tudor/letter/queen-catherine-howard-master-thomas-culpeper/, February 4, 2015

Harrison, G. B., (ed.) (1968). *The Letters of Queen Elizabeth I.* New York: Funk & Wagnalls.

*Loach, Jennifer (1999). Edward VI. New Haven, CT: Yale University Press.*

Michael K. Jones and Malcolm G. Underwood, "Beaufort, Margaret, Countess of Richmond and Derby (1443–1509)", Oxford Dictionary of National Biography, Oxford University Press, 2004

Nichols, John Gough (1850). The chronicle of Queen Jane, and of two years of Queen Mary, and especially of the rebellion of Sir Thomas Wyat. London: J. B. Nichols.

Porter, Linda (2010). *Mary Tudor: The First Queen.*

Prescott, H. F. M. (2012). *Mary Tudor.* Hatchette UK.

Stone, Jane Mary (1901). *The History of Mary I: Queen of England.* Sands & Co.

*Skidmore, Chris (2007). Edward VI: The Lost King of England. London: Weidenfeld & Nicolson.*

Mumby, Frank Arthur; "The Youth of Henry VIII – A Narrative in Contemporary Letters

Letters and Papers, Foreign and Domestic, Henry VIII, Volume 17, 1542. Originally published by Her Majesty's Stationery Office, London, 1900.

Watkins, Sarah-Beth (2017) *Margaret Tudor, Queen of Scots.* John Hunt Publishing.

# Free Bonus from Captivating History (Available for a Limited time)

Hi History Lovers!

Now you have a chance to join our exclusive history list so you can get your first history ebook for free as well as discounts and a potential to get more history books for free! Simply visit the link below to join.

Captivatinghistory.com/ebook

Also, make sure to follow us on:

Twitter: @Captivhistory

Facebook: Captivating History:@captivatinghistory

Printed in Great Britain
by Amazon